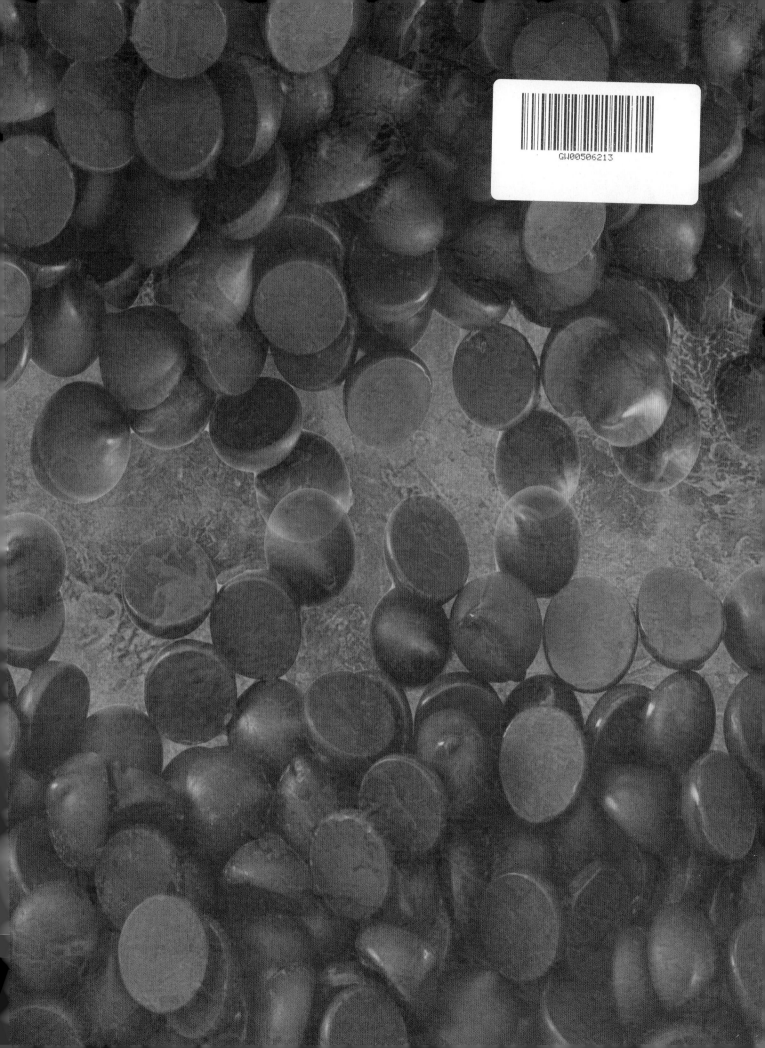

Sam

20 Aug '09

BEYOND *chips*

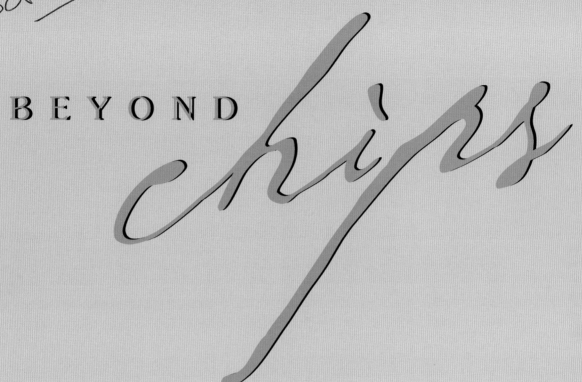

Congrats on your A Levels and
getting into Aber! We hope this
book helps you through your days
at uni and life after, I thought
it a perfect gift for our chocoholic
nephew ——

All our love

Derek, Jemma + Emilia

xxx

A Collection of
chocolate recipes from IBMers
Around the World

BEYOND *chips*
A Collection of *chocolate recipes*
from IBMers Around the World

Published by IBM Club

IBM
cl b

New Orchard Road
Armonk, New York 10504-1722

Library of Congress Control Number:
    2007931653
ISBN: 978-0-9794356-0-7

Edited, Designed, and Manufactured by
Favorite Recipes® Press
An imprint of

FRP.

P.O. Box 305142
Nashville, Tennessee 37230
800-358-0560

Art Director: Steve Newman
Book Design: Starletta Polster
Project Manager: Debbie Van Mol
Project Editor: Jane Hinshaw

Manufactured in China
First Printing: 2007
10,000 copies

*The Quarter Century Club,
which recognizes employees
with twenty-five years of
service, is organized in
1924 with a meeting held in
Atlantic City, New Jersey.*

BEYOND *chips*

A Collection of
chocolate recipes from IBMers
Around the World

CONTENTS

Foreword   6
Preface   8

cakes   10

candies   56

cookies   82

pies & pastries 110

desserts 134

brunch, snacks & beverages 162

Acknowledgments 185
Contributors 186
Index 188
Order Information 192

foreword

In the late 1920s, employees at the IBM plant in Endicott, New York, decided to form an IBM Study Club to stimulate interest in educational programs. From these modest beginnings, a global IBM Club arose, but from that time to this, the same mission exists: to make IBM a stronger company by promoting the welfare of its employees.

That mission has remained strong through various permutations of the club. In the early years, for example, the club was mostly centered in Westchester County, New York, and IBMers' calendars were packed with sports leagues and family days, among other things. These days, the club reaches around the world, representing over 140 locations in over 30 countries. Collectively, these clubs plan over 3,000 events—both large and small—each year.

Much as the IBM Clubs link employees through social gatherings and cultural events, our values link each of us to a common purpose and guide the work that we do every day. IBM's values are:

Dedication to every client's success

Innovation that matters—for our company and for the world

Trust and personal responsibility in all relationships

To celebrate the important place that the IBM Club has played in IBM's history and in furthering IBM's values, I am pleased to present *Beyond Chips—A Collection of Chocolate Recipes from IBMers Around the World*, an IBM Club Heritage Cookbook.

Richard Calo

Richard Calo
Vice President, Global Workforce Relations

1890 Dey Time Recorder
One of the three companies that merged to
form the C-T-R (Computing-Tabulating-Recording)
Company in 1911 was the International Time
Recording Company, originally known as
the Bundy Manufacturing Company, which
manufactured a variety of time recording devices.

In 1911, financier Charles R. Flint
directed the merger of the
International Time Recording
Company, the Computing Scale
Company, and the Tabulating
Machine Company to form the
Computing-Tabulating-Recording
Company (CTR). In 1914, Thomas
J. Watson, Sr., was named general
manager of CTR.

1914 Time Recording Products

In 1924, the Computing-Tabulating-Recording
Company adopted the name International
Business Machines Corporation. The ornate
letters that formed the "CTR" logo were
replaced by the words "Business Machines"
in more contemporary sans serif type, and in
a form intended to suggest a globe, girdled
by the word "International."

preface

Working at IBM means having more than 350,000 co-workers—a number that can seem a bit overwhelming. Fortunately for IBMers, the IBM Club brings employees and retirees, as well as their families, together outside of work to participate in social, cultural, or recreational activities. From the positive response to the IBM Club programs, it would seem that employees agree that a good way to get to know more colleagues is to find similar interests outside of work. With such a broadly diverse employee population, there is usually something for everyone—from book clubs and music groups to hiking and yoga classes, from day trips to local attractions to sports leagues, and much more.

IBM Clubs have recently expanded to serve employees who are mobile, who travel, or who just have a desire to connect with co-workers with specific interests. Members can take advantage of the IBM Club Web site, learn what's going on in clubs around the world, participate in any global or online events, and access discount information. For travelers, there are more than 150 IBMers all over the world who have volunteered to inform employees about club activities that are happening at their destinations. And, members are encouraged to create new events and cultivate new local interests to strengthen the presence of the club both locally and worldwide.

The IBM Clubs' continued growth is possible because of the spirit and enthusiasm of the 140,000 members worldwide. This book is dedicated to each one of them.

Sue Cutrone

Sue Cutrone
Global IBM Club Program Manager

1933 Tabulator

Before punched cards could be used by other machines to produce finished printed reports, they had to be sorted into desired classifications and placed into proper numerical sequence. IBM Electric Punched Card Sorting Machines, like this one in 1938, did this automatically.

In the early 1960s, IBM's Burlington, Vermont, facility becomes the production center for American Airlines SABRE, the first fully computerized reservation system.

Within eight months of its opening in 1967, IBM's Austin, Texas, plant was manufacturing three products. In addition to the Selectric Composer, the site also produced the IBM Magnetic Tape Selectric Composer (MTSC) and IBM Magnetic Tape Selectric Typewriter (MTST) pictured here. All three products had been announced by Office Products Division prior to the opening of the Austin facility, and manufacturing responsibility for them was transferred from Lexington, Kentucky, to Austin.

cakes

This 300-pound five-foot-high anniversary cake was presented to Mr. and Mrs. Thomas J. Watson, Sr., at the Fortieth Anniversary Dinner, April 30, 1954, in New York City. Over 350 tribute dinners were held in fifty-seven countries to honor Thomas J. Watson, Sr., on his fortieth anniversary with IBM.

RECOGNITION EVENTS

When looking for the reasons for IBM's continued success, look no further than our extraordinary employees. Over the years, IBM has sustained an ongoing commitment to recognizing excellence and experience wherever it might be found in the company. From honoring extended tenures with the Quarter Century Club to celebrating sales achievements with the Hundred Percent Club, just two of the many examples available, IBM has a history of employee recognition that continues to this day.

Fudgy Chocolate Layer Cake 14

Mocha Layer Cake 15

Swiss Chocolate Torte 16

Torta al Cioccolato 17

Caprese 17

Creole Chocolate Cake 18

Chocolate Cake 19

Sour Cream Chocolate Chip
Cake 19

Cupavci 20

Chocolate Crazy Cake 20

Devil's Black Cake 21

Intensely Rich
Chocolate Cake 22

Flourless Chocolate Cake 23

Frozen Chocolate Cake 23

Chocolate Mousse Cake 24

Rich Chocolate Cake 25

Indian Chocolate Cake 26

Sugar-Free Chocolate Cake 27

Chocolate Torte 28

Fabulous Chocolate-Chocolate
Chip Cake 29

Black Russian Cake 29

Chocolate Coconut Fudge Ring
Bundt Cake 30

Vanilla Wafer Cake 30

Chocolate Bundt Cake 31

Prestigio Cake 32

Mocha Bundt Cake 32

Vodka Cake 33

Black Forest Cake 33

Chocolate Cherry Cake 34

Chocolate Mocha Cake 35

Chocolate Chip Cake 35

Oatmeal Chocolate
Chip Cake 36

Chocolate Chip
Zucchini Cake 36

Frosted Chocolate Cake 37

Chocolate Cinnamon
Snacking Cake 38

Earthquake Cake 38

Hot Fudge
Chocolate Cake 40

Heavenly Cake 41

Mississippi Mud Cake 42

One-Pan Peanut Butter
Chocolate Cake 43

Screwball Dark
Chocolate Cake 43

Wacky Cake 44

Navy Cake 46

Chocolate Syrup Cake 46

Triple Chocolate Cake 47

Chocolate Sheet Cake 47

Texas Sheet Cake 49

Amazingly Rich Individual
Chocolate Pudding Cakes 50

Chocolate Lava Cakes 51

Chocolate Cherry Cupcakes 51

Macaroon-Filled Chocolate
Cupcakes 52

Surprise Cupcakes 54

Fudge Frosting 54

Chocolate Peanut Butter
Frosting 55

FUDGY CHOCOLATE LAYER CAKE

Cake
3/4 cup (1 1/2 sticks) butter
2 ounces unsweetened
    baking chocolate
2 1/4 cups all-purpose flour
2 cups sugar
1/4 cup baking cocoa
2 teaspoons baking soda
1 teaspoon salt
1 3/4 cups buttermilk
2 eggs

Creamy Frosting
3/4 cup whipping cream
1 1/2 cups (9 ounces) semisweet
    chocolate chips

Cake

Combine the butter and chocolate in a small saucepan. Heat over low heat until melted, stirring to blend well. Mix the flour, sugar, baking cocoa, baking soda and salt in a large mixing bowl. Add the melted chocolate mixture, buttermilk and eggs. Beat at low speed for 1 minute. Increase the speed to high and beat for 2 minutes or until light and fluffy.

Spoon the batter into two greased and floured 9-inch cake pans. Bake in a preheated 350-degree oven for 25 to 30 minutes or until the layers spring back when lightly touched. Cool in the pans for 5 minutes and invert onto wire racks to cool completely.

Frosting

Bring the cream just to a simmer in a saucepan and remove from the heat. Add the chocolate chips and stir until the chips melt and the frosting is thickened and smooth.

Place one cake layer on a cake plate and spread with 1/3 cup of the frosting. Top with the remaining cake layer and spread the remaining frosting over the top and side.

You can melt the butter and chocolate in the microwave for 1 to 2 minutes if you prefer.

Serves 8

MOCHA LAYER CAKE

Cake

Mix the flour, baking powder, baking soda and baking cocoa in a bowl. Mix the coffee, milk and vanilla in a small bowl. Cream the butter with the sugar in a mixing bowl until light and fluffy. Beat in the eggs. Add the dry ingredients alternately with the coffee mixture, beating at medium speed for 2 minutes.

Spoon the batter into two greased and floured 9-inch cake pans. Bake in a preheated 375-degree oven for 20 to 25 minutes or until the layers test done. Cool in the pans on a wire rack for 10 minutes and remove to the wire rack to cool completely.

Frosting

Cream the butter in a mixing bowl. Add the confectioners' sugar, baking cocoa and salt and beat until light. Add the coffee and vanilla and beat until of spreading consistency. Spread between the layers and over the top and side of the cake.

You can also bake this in a 9×13-inch cake pan for 30 to 35 minutes. You will need only half the frosting recipe to frost the cake. The recipe has been adjusted for altitudes above 6,000 feet.

Serves 12

Cake

2 cups plus 2 tablespoons
    all-purpose flour
1 teaspoon baking powder
1 teaspoon baking soda
3/4 cup baking cocoa
1 cup cold brewed coffee
1 cup milk
1 teaspoon vanilla extract
1/2 cup (1 stick) butter, softened
2 cups sugar
2 eggs

Mocha Frosting

1/3 cup butter, softened
3 cups confectioners' sugar
1/2 cup baking cocoa
1/4 teaspoon salt
1/3 cup (or less) cold brewed coffee
1/2 teaspoon vanilla extract

Thomas J. Watson, Sr., Tribute Dinner, Cairo, Egypt, April 1954.

SWISS CHOCOLATE TORTE

Torte

1 (2-layer) package Swiss chocolate
   or devil's food cake mix
1 (4-ounce) package vanilla instant
   pudding mix
3 eggs
1 1/4 cups milk
1/2 cup vegetable oil

Almond Crunch Frosting

8 ounces cream cheese, softened
1 cup confectioners' sugar
1 cup granulated sugar
8 (1 1/2-ounce) chocolate candy bars
   with almonds, chopped
16 ounces whipped topping
2 (1 1/2-ounce) chocolate candy bars
   with almonds, chopped

Torte

Sift the cake mix and the pudding mix into a large mixing bowl. Combine the eggs, milk and oil in a bowl and whisk to mix well. Add to the cake mix mixture and beat until smooth.

Spoon the batter into three greased and floured 9-inch cake pans. Bake in a preheated 350-degree oven for 20 to 25 minutes or until wooden picks inserted near the centers come out clean. Cool in the pans for 10 minutes and invert onto wire racks to cool completely.

Frosting

Beat the cream cheese with the confectioners' sugar and granulated sugar in a mixing bowl until light and fluffy. Stir in 8 chopped candy bars. Fold in the whipped topping.

Spread a layer of frosting the size of the cake layer on a cake plate and place one cake layer on the plate. Stack the remaining cake layers on the plate, spreading the remaining frosting between the layers and over the top and side of the cake. Sprinkle 2 chopped candy bars over the top and around the bottom edge of the cake. Place in an airtight container and chill in the refrigerator for 8 hours or longer.

Serves 12

TORTA AL CIOCCOLATO

Combine the chocolate and butter in a double boiler and heat over simmering water until melted, stirring to blend well. Combine the eggs, sugar and flour in a bowl and mix well. Add the chocolate mixture and mix until smooth.

Spoon the batter into a baking parchment-lined 9-inch (24-centimeter) springform pan. Bake in a preheated 350-degree (175-degree C) oven for 25 minutes or until the torte tests done and has a strong chocolate aroma. Cool in the pan on a wire rack. Place on a serving dish and remove the side of the pan to serve.

Serves 8

7.1 ounces (200 grams) dark chocolate
5.3 ounces (150 grams) butter
4 medium eggs
5.3 ounces (150 grams) sugar
1.8 ounces (50 grams) all-purpose flour

CAPRESE

Grind the almonds with the sugar. Combine the chocolate and butter in a saucepan and melt over low heat, stirring to blend well. Combine the almond mixture, chocolate mixture, eggs, flavorings and salt in a bowl; beat until smooth.

Spoon the batter into a buttered and floured 9-inch cake pan. Bake in a preheated 400-degree (200-degree C) oven for 10 minutes. Reduce the oven temperature to 350 degrees (170 degrees C) and bake for 30 to 40 minutes longer or until the cake tests done. Cool in the pan for several minutes and remove to a wire rack to cool completely.

This flourless cake from the Isle of Capri is a good choice for those who can't eat wheat products. For a softer cake, beat the egg whites separately and fold them into the batter at the end.

Serves 8 to 10

8 ounces (200 grams) shelled almonds
8 ounces (200 grams) superfine sugar
8 ounces (200 grams) dark chocolate
1 cup (200 grams/2 sticks) butter
5 eggs, beaten
1 tablespoon vanilla extract, or the seeds of 1 vanilla bean
2 teaspoons almond extract, or 5 ground bitter almonds
Pinch of salt

CREOLE CHOCOLATE CAKE

12 ounces bittersweet chocolate
1 cup sugar
1/2 cup bourbon
1 cup (2 sticks) butter, chopped
    and softened
6 eggs, at room temperature
11/2 tablespoons all-purpose flour
1/2 cup sugar
2 cups sliced fresh strawberries
1 cup whipped cream
Mint leaves, for garnish

Chop the chocolate into 1/4-inch pieces and place in a stainless steel mixing bowl. Place 1 inch of water in a saucepan and bring to a simmer. Place the mixing bowl in the saucepan and heat until the chocolate melts, stirring occasionally.

Combine 1 cup sugar with the bourbon in a saucepan. Bring just to a low boil, stirring occasionally to dissolve the sugar. Pour over the chocolate and stir to blend well. Remove from the heat and stir in the butter.

Combine the eggs with the flour and 1/2 cup sugar in a stainless steel mixing bowl and beat at high speed for 5 minutes. Fold into the chocolate mixture with a rubber spatula, incorporating well.

Butter a 9-inch springform pan and line the bottom with baking parchment. Cover the outside of the springform pan with foil, sealing tightly. Spoon the batter into the prepared pan and place in a larger shallow baking pan. Pour 1 inch of water in the larger pan. Bake in a preheated 375-degree oven for 1 hour. Remove from the pan of water and cool in the springform pan on a wire rack for 1 hour. Cover with plastic wrap and chill in the refrigerator for 4 hours or longer. Place on a serving plate and remove the side of the pan. Top with the strawberries and whipped cream; garnish with mint leaves.

In Louisiana, this is a popular Creole dessert.

Serves 8 to 10

CHOCOLATE CAKE

Place the chocolate in a small heatproof bowl and place over simmering water in a saucepan. Heat until the chocolate melts, taking care not to let any water reach the chocolate. Melt the butter in a small saucepan. Add the butter to the chocolate and blend well.

Add the sugar and mix well. Beat in the egg yolks. Add the flour gradually, beating until smooth. Beat the egg whites in a mixing bowl until soft peaks form. Fold into the chocolate mixture.

Spoon the batter into a buttered and floured cake pan. Bake in a preheated 400-degree (200-degree C) oven for 10 to 15 minutes or until the cake tests done. Cool in the pan for 5 minutes and remove to a wire rack to cool completely.

Serves 6 to 8

12 ounces dark chocolate
6 ounces butter
3/4 cup sugar
6 egg yolks
3 tablespoons all-purpose flour
6 egg whites

SOUR CREAM CHOCOLATE CHIP CAKE

Toss the chocolate chips with a small amount of the cake flour. Sift the remaining cake flour with the baking powder and baking soda. Blend the sour cream and vanilla in a bowl.

Cream the butter and sugar in a mixing bowl until light and fluffy. Beat in the eggs. Add the dry ingredients alternately with the sour cream mixture, mixing well after each addition. Stir in the chocolate chips.

Spoon the batter into a greased and floured 8×8-inch cake pan. Bake in a preheated 350-degree oven for 40 minutes. Cool in the pan for 5 minutes and remove to a wire rack to cool completely.

Serves 8

1 cup (6 ounces) chocolate chips
2 cups cake flour
1 teaspoon baking powder
1 teaspoon baking soda
1 cup sour cream
1 teaspoon vanilla extract
1/2 cup (1 stick) butter or
    margarine, softened
1 cup sugar
2 eggs, beaten

CUPAVCI

Cake

4 eggs
1 1/2 cups sugar
1 1/2 cups vegetable oil
1 1/2 cups milk
1 1/2 cups all-purpose flour
1 tablespoon baking powder

Chocolate Coconut Coating

1 cup milk
6 ounces baking chocolate
8 ounces butter
Flaked coconut

Cake

Combine the eggs and sugar in a mixing bowl and beat until smooth. Add the oil and mix well. Add the milk, flour and baking powder in that order and beat until smooth after each addition.

Spoon the batter into a greased and floured square cake pan. Bake in a preheated 400-degree (200-degree C) oven for 25 minutes. Cool the cake in the pan. Cut the cake into squares.

Coating

Combine the milk, chocolate and butter in a saucepan and heat until the chocolate and butter melt, stirring to blend well; do not allow to boil. Dip the cake squares into the chocolate mixture and coat evenly with coconut.

This recipe comes from Croatia, and the name means "furry," because of the coconut. In northern Croatia, they sometimes add honey to the cake and rum to the chocolate sauce.

Serves 9

CHOCOLATE CRAZY CAKE

1 1/2 cups all-purpose flour
1 cup sugar
1/2 teaspoon baking soda
1/2 teaspoon salt
3 tablespoons baking cocoa
1/3 cup vegetable oil
1 1/2 tablespoons vinegar
1/2 teaspoon vanilla extract
1 cup cold water

Combine the flour, sugar, baking soda, salt, baking cocoa, oil, vinegar, vanilla and water in an 8×8-inch cake pan and mix by hand until smooth. Bake in a preheated 350-degree oven for 30 minutes or until the cake tests done.

Serves 9

DEVIL'S BLACK CAKE

Mix the rice flour with the cornstarch, baking powder, baking soda and salt. Combine the baking cocoa with the water and vanilla in a bowl and mix well.

Cream the butter in a mixing bowl until light. Add the sugar gradually, beating constantly until fluffy. Beat in the eggs one at a time. Add the dry ingredients alternately with the chocolate mixture, mixing well after each addition.

Butter a 10-inch cake pan with a 3-inch side. Sprinkle with additional rice flour. Spoon the batter into the prepared pan. Bake in a preheated 345-degree (175-degree C) oven for 35 to 40 minutes or until a wooden pick inserted near the center comes out clean. Cool in the pan for 5 minutes and remove to a wire rack to cool completely. Top with dulce de leche or any sweet cream and cover with chocolate fudge sauce and chopped nuts.

This cake, made with rice flour, is a good choice for those allergic to wheat products.

Serves 10

1^1/2 cups rice flour
^{1}/2 cup cornstarch
1^1/4 teaspoons baking powder
^{1}/2 teaspoon baking soda
^{3}/4 teaspoon salt
^{1}/2 cup baking cocoa
1 cup water
^{1}/2 teaspoon vanilla extract
^{1}/2 cup (1 stick) butter, softened
1^1/4 cups sugar
2 eggs
Dulce de leche
Chocolate fudge sauce
Chopped nuts

On a cold day in February 1955, members of the early reception committee served refreshing snacks and hot beverages to the 1954 Hundred Percent Club conventioneers arriving at the train station in Chicago, Illinois.

INTENSELY RICH CHOCOLATE CAKE

Chocolate Wafer Crust
20 chocolate wafers
3 tablespoons butter, melted

Cake
12 ounces semisweet
    baking chocolate
3/4 cup (1 1/2 sticks) butter
6 egg yolks
6 tablespoons sugar
2 teaspoons vanilla extract
6 egg whites
6 tablespoons sugar

Chocolate Glaze
6 ounces semisweet
    baking chocolate
2 tablespoons butter
3 tablespoons milk
2 tablespoons light corn syrup

Garnish
3 ounces semisweet
    baking chocolate
Confectioners' sugar

Crust
Place the chocolate wafers in a plastic bag and crush to fine crumbs using a rolling pin. Mix with the butter in a bowl. Press over the bottom of a 9-inch springform pan sprayed with nonstick cooking spray.

Cake
Melt the chocolate with the butter in a small saucepan over low heat, stirring occasionally to blend well. Remove from the heat and let cool slightly, stirring occasionally.

Beat the egg yolks at high speed in a mixing bowl until light and foamy. Add 6 tablespoons sugar and beat for 3 minutes or until thick and pale yellow. Add the chocolate mixture and beat at low speed to mix well. Blend in the vanilla.

Beat the egg whites with clean dry beaters in a mixing bowl until soft peaks form. Add 6 tablespoons sugar 1 tablespoon at a time, beating constantly until stiff peaks form. Fold into the chocolate mixture.

Pour the batter into the prepared crust. Bake in a preheated 350-degree oven for 45 to 50 minutes or until the top is puffed and cracked. Cool in the pan on a wire rack. Loosen from the side of the pan with a knife and remove the side of the pan. Place a sheet of baking parchment or waxed paper under the rack.

Glaze
Melt the chocolate and butter in a saucepan over very low heat, stirring occasionally until smooth. Remove from the heat and stir in the milk and corn syrup. Spread evenly over the top and side of the cake. Chill for 30 minutes or until the glaze is almost set.

Garnish
Line a large baking sheet with baking parchment or waxed paper. Melt the chocolate and pour into a 10-inch circle on the baking sheet. Place in the freezer for 5 minutes or until firm. Break into large pieces. Sprinkle the chocolate pieces and the top of the cake with confectioners' sugar. Arrange the chocolate pieces over the top of the cake. Chill for up to 1 hour before serving.

Serves 18

FLOURLESS CHOCOLATE CAKE

Melt the chocolate with the butter in a double boiler over simmering heat, stirring to blend well. Remove from the heat and whisk in the sugar substitute. Whisk in the eggs one at a time. Add the baking cocoa and vanilla and whisk until smooth. Butter an 8-inch cake pan and line with buttered baking parchment. Spoon the batter into the prepared pan. Bake in a preheated 375-degree oven for 25 minutes or until the top forms a thin crust. Cool in the pan on a wire rack for 5 minutes. Invert onto a serving plate. Top the servings with the mixed berries and garnish with toasted almonds, whipped cream or confectioners' sugar.

Serves 10

4 ounces bittersweet
  chocolate, chopped
1/2 cup (1 stick) unsalted butter
3/4 cup sugar substitute
3 eggs
1/2 cup baking cocoa
1 teaspoon vanilla extract
3/4 cup mixed berries
Toasted almonds, whipped cream or
  confectioners' sugar, for garnish

FROZEN CHOCOLATE CAKE

Melt the chocolate with the butter in a double boiler over simmering water, stirring to blend well. Cool to room temperature. Beat the egg yolks with the sugar in a mixing bowl until thick and pale yellow. Add the chocolate mixture and mix well. Beat the egg whites in a mixing bowl until stiff peaks form. Fold into the chocolate mixture. Reserve 1 cup of the batter.

Spoon the remaining batter into a buttered 9-inch cake pan. Bake in a preheated 350-degree (180-degree C) oven for 45 minutes or until a wooden pick inserted near the center comes out clean. Cool in the pan on a wire rack. Beat the whipping cream in a mixing bowl until soft peaks form. Fold in the reserved cake batter. Spread over the cooled cake and garnish with chocolate curls. Freeze until serving time.

If you are concerned about using raw eggs, use eggs pasteurized in their shells, which are sold at some specialty food stores, or use an equivalent amount of pasteurized egg substitute.

Serves 8

6 ounces (170 grams) unsweetened
  baking chocolate
3 ounces (85 grams) unsalted butter
6 egg yolks
4 ounces (120 grams) sugar
6 egg whites
1 cup (250 grams) heavy
  whipping cream
Chocolate curls, for garnish

CHOCOLATE MOUSSE CAKE

Cake

1 cup (4 ounces) whole hazelnuts
3 tablespoons butter or margarine, melted
16 ounces semisweet chocolate, chopped
1/2 cup heavy whipping cream
6 eggs
1 teaspoon vanilla extract
1/3 cup all-purpose flour
1/4 cup sugar
1/2 cup heavy whipping cream

Chocolate Whipped Cream

1/2 cup heavy whipping cream
1/2 ounce semisweet chocolate

Cake

Grind the hazelnuts in a food processor or blender; the ground nuts should measure about 1 1/4 cups. Mix with the butter in a bowl. Press over the bottom and 1 1/2 inches up the side of a greased 9-inch springform pan.

Combine the chocolate with 1/2 cup cream in a saucepan. Heat over low heat until the chocolate melts, stirring to blend well. Remove from the heat.

Beat the eggs with the vanilla in a mixing bowl. Add the flour and sugar and beat at high speed for 10 minutes or until thick and pale yellow. Stir one-fourth of the batter into the chocolate mixture; then fold the remaining batter into the chocolate mixture. Beat 1/2 cup cream in a mixing bowl just until soft peaks form. Fold into the batter.

Spoon into the prepared pan. Bake in a preheated 325-degree oven for 30 to 35 minutes or until the outer one-third of the top is puffed but the center is still slightly soft. Cool in the pan on a wire rack for 20 minutes. Place on a serving plate and remove the side of the pan. Cool for 3 to 4 hours longer. Serve chilled or at room temperature with Chocolate Whipped Cream.

Whipped Cream

Combine the cream with the chocolate in a small saucepan. Heat over low heat until the chocolate melts, stirring to blend well. Remove from the heat and continue to stir until the chocolate is completely blended. Pour into a bowl and chill in the refrigerator. Beat the mixture until firm peaks form.

Serves 12

RICH CHOCOLATE CAKE

Cake

Beat the eggs with the sugar in a mixing bowl until foamy. Add the flour, baking cocoa, baking powder, oil and vanilla and mix until smooth.

Spoon the batter into a greased 6-inch cake pan. Bake in a preheated 350-degree (180-degree C) oven for 30 minutes or until a wooden pick inserted near the center comes out clean. Cool in the pan for 5 minutes and remove to a wire rack to cool completely. Cut the cake horizontally into two layers and level the top if necessary for a flat surface.

Frosting

Combine the cream with the chocolate in a saucepan. Heat until the chocolate melts, stirring to blend well. Chill in the refrigerator until thickened. Spread one-third of the mixture between the cake layers. Spread the remaining frosting over the top and side of the cake. Chill in the refrigerator for 1 hour or until the frosting is set. Serve at room temperature.

Serves 4

Cake

4 eggs
3/4 cup (120 grams) sugar
1 cup (125 grams) all-purpose flour
1 tablespoon baking cocoa
1 1/4 teaspoons baking powder
1/4 cup vegetable oil
1 tablespoon vanilla extract

Chocolate Cream Frosting

1/2 cup heavy cream
1 cup (150 grams) semisweet
   chocolate

INDIAN CHOCOLATE CAKE

5 ounces (150 grams/1¼ cups)
  self-rising flour, sifted
1 teaspoon baking cocoa
1 teaspoon chocolate powder, or
  1 additional teaspoon
  baking cocoa
1 teaspoon baking powder
½ teaspoon baking soda
1 ounce (30 grams) roasted
  cashews, broken
½ (14-ounce) can sweetened
  condensed milk
¼ cup (75 milliliters) water
½ cup (100 milliliters/1 stick)
  butter or margarine, melted
1 teaspoon vanilla extract or
  other flavoring

Combine the flour with the baking cocoa, chocolate powder, baking powder, baking soda and cashews in a mixing bowl. Add the condensed milk, water, butter and vanilla and mix well.

Spoon the batter into a greased 6- or 7-inch cake pan. Bake in a preheated 400-degree (200-degree C) oven for 10 minutes. Reduce the oven temperature to 350 degrees (180 degrees C).

Bake for 10 minutes longer or until the cake pulls from the side of the pan and the top springs back when lightly touched. Cool in the pan for 1 to 2 minutes. Invert onto a wire rack to cool completely.

Serves 5

Hundred Percent Club members, Tokyo, Japan, 1956.

SUGAR-FREE CHOCOLATE CAKE

Cake

Mix the flour, baking powder, baking soda and salt together. Combine the margarine, preserves, egg and sugar substitute in a medium mixing bowl and beat until smooth. Mix the milk and baking cocoa in a measuring cup until smooth. Add the dry ingredients to the batter alternately with the milk mixture, beginning and ending with the dry ingredients and mixing well after each addition.

Spoon the batter into a greased and floured 8-inch cake pan. Bake in a preheated 350-degree oven for 20 minutes or until a wooden pick inserted near the center comes out clean. Cool in the pan on a wire rack for 5 minutes and remove to the wire rack to cool completely. Place on a serving plate.

Glaze

Heat the milk in a small saucepan until very hot but not boiling. Remove from the heat and add the chopped chocolate, stirring until melted and blended. Stir in the sugar substitute. Cook over low heat until smooth, stirring constantly. Cool to room temperature and chill in the refrigerator for 15 minutes or until thickened enough to spread. Spread over the cake and chill for 15 to 20 minutes or until the glaze is firm. Drizzle the melted chocolate over the top in a lacy pattern. Chill for 10 minutes or until firm.

Serves 8

Cake

1 cup all-purpose flour
1 teaspoon baking powder
1/2 teaspoon baking soda
1/4 teaspoon salt
1/4 cup (1/2 stick) margarine, softened
1/4 cup light raspberry preserves or spreadable raspberry fruit
1 egg
24 envelopes sugar substitute
1/2 cup skim milk
3 tablespoons Dutch-process or European-process baking cocoa

Chocolate Glaze

1/3 cup skim milk
3 ounces unsweetened baking chocolate, chopped
18 envelopes sugar substitute
1/2 to 1 ounce unsweetened baking chocolate, melted

CHOCOLATE TORTE

1 tablespoon margarine, softened
1/3 cup finely ground nuts, such as
    walnuts or Brazil nuts
1 teaspoon instant espresso
    granules, or 2 teaspoons instant
    coffee granules
2 tablespoons hot water
4 egg yolks
1/4 cup granulated sugar
3 ounces bittersweet chocolate or
    semisweet chocolate, melted
    and cooled
4 egg whites
1/4 cup granulated sugar
Confectioners' sugar
Chocolate curls, for garnish

Spread the margarine over the bottom and 11/2 inches up the side of
a 9-inch springform pan. Reserve 1 or 2 tablespoons of the ground
nuts. Sprinkle the remaining nuts in the springform pan.

Dissolve the espresso granules in the hot water in a small bowl.
Beat the egg yolks at high speed in a medium mixing bowl for
5 minutes or until thick and pale yellow. Beat in 1/4 cup granulated
sugar gradually. Beat in the melted chocolate at low speed. Add the
dissolved espresso and beat until smooth.

Beat the egg whites in a large mixing bowl until soft peaks form.
Add 1/4 cup granulated sugar gradually, beating constantly until stiff
peaks form. Fold gently into the chocolate mixture.

Spread evenly in the prepared pan. Bake in a preheated 350-degree
oven for 20 to 25 minutes or until set. Cool in the pan on a wire
rack for 15 minutes; the center will fall slightly and the edge will be
crumbly. Place on a serving plate and loosen from the pan with a
thin metal spatula. Remove the side of the pan and cool completely.

Serve right away or chill in the refrigerator for up to 24 hours.
Let stand until at room temperature to serve. Dust the servings
with confectioners' sugar and the reserved nuts. Garnish with
chocolate curls.

Serves 10

Fabulous Chocolate-Chocolate Chip Cake

Combine the cake mix, pudding mix, sour cream, shortening, eggs and water in a mixing bowl. Beat at medium speed until smooth. Stir in the chocolate chips.

Spoon the batter into a greased and floured 10-inch bundt pan. Bake in a preheated 350-degree oven for 45 to 55 minutes or until a wooden pick inserted near the center comes out clean. Cool in the pan for 20 minutes and invert onto a wire rack to cool completely. Garnish with confectioners' sugar and/or serve with vanilla ice cream.

Serves 10 to 12

1 (2-layer) package chocolate fudge or devil's food cake mix
1 package chocolate instant pudding mix
1 cup sour cream
1/2 cup shortening or vegetable oil
4 eggs
1/2 cup water
1 1/2 cups (9 ounces) chocolate chips
Confectioners' sugar, for garnish

Black Russian Cake

Cake
Combine the cake mix, pudding mix, sugar, oil, water, Kahlúa, vodka and eggs in a mixing bowl. Mix at low speed for 3 minutes or until smooth.

Pour the batter into a bundt pan that has been greased and floured or sprayed with nonstick cooking spray. Bake in a preheated 350-degree oven for 55 to 70 minutes or until the cake tests done. Cool in the pan for 5 minutes and invert onto a serving plate to cool completely.

Glaze
Combine the confectioners' sugar and Kahlúa in a bowl and mix until smooth. Brush over the cake. Serve with vanilla ice cream, if desired. Store for up to 1 week.

Serves 16

Cake
1 (2-layer) package yellow cake mix without pudding
1 (6-ounce) package chocolate instant pudding mix
1 cup sugar
1 cup vegetable oil
3/4 cup water
1/4 cup Kahlúa
1/4 cup vodka
4 eggs

Kahlúa Glaze
1/2 cup confectioners' sugar
1/4 cup Kahlúa

CHOCOLATE COCONUT FUDGE RING BUNDT CAKE

Coconut Chocolate Chip Filling

8 ounces cream cheese, softened
1/4 cup sugar
1 teaspoon vanilla extract
1 egg
1/2 cup flaked coconut
1 cup (6 ounces) semisweet or milk
    chocolate chips

Cake

2 cups sugar
1 cup vegetable oil
2 eggs
3 3/4 cups sifted all-purpose flour
3/4 cup baking cocoa
1 teaspoon baking powder
2 teaspoons baking soda
1 cup hot coffee or hot water
1 cup buttermilk
1 teaspoon vanilla extract
1/2 cup chopped nuts (optional)

Filling

Beat the cream cheese, sugar and vanilla in a mixing bowl until light. Beat in the egg. Stir in the coconut and chocolate chips.

Cake

Combine the sugar, oil and eggs in a mixing bowl. Beat at high speed for 1 minute. Add the flour, baking cocoa, baking powder, baking soda, coffee, buttermilk and vanilla. Beat at medium speed for 3 minutes. Stir in the nuts.

Spread half the batter in a greased and floured 10-inch bundt pan or tube pan. Spoon the filling carefully over the batter. Top with the remaining batter. Bake in a preheated 350-degree oven for 1 hour and 10 minutes to 1 hour and 15 minutes or until the top springs back when lightly touched. Cool upright in the pan for 15 minutes. Invert onto a wire rack to cool completely.

Serves 12

VANILLA WAFER CAKE

2 1/4 cups crushed vanilla wafers
1 cup coconut
1 cup chopped nuts
1/2 cup (1 stick) margarine, softened
1 cup sugar
3 eggs
1/3 cup milk
1/3 cup (2 ounces) chocolate chips

Mix the crushed vanilla wafers, coconut and nuts in a bowl. Cream the margarine and sugar in a mixing bowl until light and fluffy. Beat in the eggs. Add the milk and mix well. Add the vanilla wafer mixture and chocolate chips and mix well. Spoon the batter into a greased and floured bundt pan. Bake in a preheated 300-degree oven for 1 hour. Cool in the pan for 15 minutes. Remove to a wire rack to cool completely.

You can also prepare this in a 9×13-inch cake pan; adjust the baking time to 20 to 30 minutes.

Serves 20 to 24

CHOCOLATE BUNDT CAKE

Topping

Combine the butter, sugar, liqueur and water in a saucepan. Heat over low heat until the butter melts and the sugar dissolves, stirring to mix well. Increase the heat and boil for 2 minutes. Let stand until cooled completely.

Cake

Combine the cake mix, pudding mix, sour cream, eggs, oil, water, liqueur and cinnamon in a mixing bowl and mix until smooth. Stir in the orange zest and chocolate chips.

Spoon the batter into a greased and floured bundt pan. Bake in a preheated 350-degree oven for 45 to 60 minutes or until a wooden pick inserted near the center comes out with a few moist crumbs. Pour the topping over the cake in the pan. Let stand on a wire rack for 30 minutes. Remove to a serving plate and cool completely. Sprinkle with confectioners' sugar.

Serves 12

Orange Topping

1/2 cup (1 stick) butter
1 cup sugar
1/4 cup orange liqueur or
    Irish whiskey
1/4 cup water

Cake

1 (2-layer) package devil's food
    cake mix
1 (4-ounce) package chocolate fudge
    instant pudding mix
1 cup sour cream
4 eggs
1/2 cup vegetable oil
1/2 cup water
1/4 cup coffee liqueur
1 teaspoon ground cinnamon
2 tablespoons grated orange zest
2 cups (12 ounces) chocolate chips
Confectioners' sugar

Thomas J. Watson, Sr., Tribute Dinner, Salvador, Brazil, April 1954.

PRESTIGIO CAKE

Cake
3 cups all-purpose flour
2 cups sugar
1 cup baking cocoa
1 tablespoon baking powder
4 eggs
1 cup vegetable oil or melted butter
1 cup hot water

Coconut Filling
1 (14-ounce) can sweetened
    condensed milk
1 package flaked coconut
1/2 cup milk

Chocolate Frosting Sauce
1 (14-ounce) can sweetened
    condensed milk
2 tablespoons unsalted butter
3 tablespoons baking cocoa
Shaved chocolate, for garnish

Cake
Sift the flour, sugar, baking cocoa and baking powder into a bowl; stir to mix well. Add the eggs, oil and water and mix until smooth.

Spoon the batter into a greased and floured bundt pan or tube pan. Bake in a preheated 350-degree oven for 40 to 45 minutes or until the cake tests done. Cool in the pan for 5 minutes and remove to a serving plate to cool completely.

Filling
Combine the condensed milk, coconut and milk in a bowl and mix well. Spoon into the center of the cake.

Sauce
Combine the condensed milk with the butter and baking cocoa in a saucepan and mix well. Cook over medium-low heat until thickened to the desired consistency, stirring to mix well. Spread over the cake and garnish with shaved chocolate.

Serves 12

MOCHA BUNDT CAKE

1 (2-layer) package chocolate
    cake mix
2 cups sour cream
2 eggs
1/2 cup Kahlúa
1/4 cup vegetable oil
1 cup (6 ounces) semisweet
    chocolate chips
1/2 cup crushed toffee bits
Confectioners' sugar

Combine the cake mix, sour cream, eggs, Kahlúa and oil in a large mixing bowl and beat until smooth. Stir in the chocolate chips and toffee bits.

Spoon the batter into a greased and floured bundt pan. Bake in a preheated 350-degree oven for 50 to 55 minutes or until the cake tests done. Cool in the pan on a wire rack for 10 to 15 minutes. Remove to the wire rack to cool completely. Sprinkle confectioners' sugar over the cake and serve with whipped cream.

Serves 10 to 12

VODKA CAKE

Combine the cake mix, pudding mixes and eggs in a large mixing bowl and mix until smooth. Add the oil, Kahlúa and vodka; mix well.

Spoon the batter into an oiled 8-cup bundt pan. Bake in a preheated 350-degree oven for 45 minutes. Cool in the pan for several minutes and remove to a serving plate. Spread the hot cake with the chocolate fudge frosting; the frosting will melt into the cake.

Serves 12

1 (2-layer) package yellow cake mix
1 (4-ounce) package chocolate instant pudding mix
1 (6-ounce) package chocolate instant pudding mix
4 eggs, at room temperature
1 cup vegetable oil
1/2 cup Kahlúa
1/2 cup vodka
1 can chocolate fudge frosting

BLACK FOREST CAKE

Combine the flour, pudding mix, sugar, baking cocoa, baking powder, baking soda and salt in a mixing bowl and mix well. Mix in the butter and flavorings. Add the eggs and buttermilk alternately, mixing well after each addition. Add the chocolate chips and pie filling and mix just until moistened.

Spoon the batter into a greased and floured 9×13-inch cake pan. Bake in a preheated 350-degree oven for 1 hour or until a wooden pick inserted near the center comes out clean. Cool in the pan on a wire rack. Serve with vanilla ice cream, if desired.

Serves 12

11/2 cups all-purpose flour
1/3 cup chocolate instant pudding mix
1 cup sugar
1/2 cup baking cocoa
2 teaspoons baking powder
1/2 teaspoon baking soda
1/2 teaspoon salt
1/2 cup (1 stick) butter, softened
1/2 teaspoon vanilla extract
1 tablespoon almond extract
3 eggs
1/2 cup buttermilk
1 cup (6 ounces) semisweet chocolate chips
1 (21-ounce) can cherry pie filling

CHOCOLATE CHERRY CAKE

Cake

1 (2-layer) package devil's food
    cake mix
1 (21-ounce) can cherry pie filling
2 eggs, beaten
1 teaspoon almond extract

Fudgy Frosting

5 tablespoons butter
1 cup sugar
1/3 cup milk
1 cup (6 ounces) chocolate chips
1 teaspoon vanilla extract

Cake

Combine the cake mix, pie filling, eggs and almond extract in a mixing bowl. Beat at medium speed for 2 minutes or until smooth.

Spoon the batter into a greased and floured 9×13-inch cake pan. Bake in a preheated 350-degree oven for 35 minutes or until a wooden pick inserted near the center comes out clean. Cool on a wire rack. You can also bake the cake in a 9×13-inch glass baking dish in a preheated 325-degree oven.

Frosting

Combine the butter, sugar and milk in a heavy saucepan and bring to a boil. Cook for 1 1/2 minutes, stirring frequently. Remove from the heat and add the chocolate chips. Beat with a spoon until the chips melt and the mixture is shiny. Stir in the vanilla and beat for 1 minute longer.

Pour over the cake immediately and quickly spread evenly; the frosting will set up very quickly and you should not touch it once it begins to set.

Serves 16

March 1967: On a trip to the Asia-Pacific area, World Trade Corporation President G. E. Jones arrived in Hong Kong in time to share in the observance of the tenth anniversary of the office. Shown here with him are W. J. Kaffer (right), General Manager of IBM Hong Kong, and three IBMers who had been with the office since its founding. From left: Kam Leung, Mrs. Ivy Woo, and John Ho.

CHOCOLATE MOCHA CAKE

Sift the flour, sugar, baking cocoa, baking powder, baking soda and salt together twice. Mix the milk and coffee in a bowl. Combine the eggs with the oil and vanilla in a mixing bowl. Mix in the sifted ingredients alternately with the coffee mixture, stirring with a large spoon as the batter becomes very thin.

Pour the batter into a greased and floured 9×13-inch cake pan. Bake in a preheated 350-degree oven for 30 minutes or until the cake tests done. Cool in the pan on a wire rack. This is a very moist cake that stores and freezes well.

Serves 15

2 cups all-purpose flour
2 cups sugar
3/4 cup baking cocoa
2 teaspoons baking powder
1 1/2 teaspoons baking soda
3/4 teaspoon salt
1 cup milk
1 cup cold strong brewed coffee
2 eggs
1/2 cup vegetable oil
1 teaspoon vanilla extract

CHOCOLATE CHIP CAKE

Combine the cake mix, pudding mix, chocolate chips, eggs, oil and water in an ungreased 9×13-inch cake pan. Mix with a fork until moistened.

Bake in a preheated 350-degree oven for 40 to 45 minutes or until the cake tests done. Cool in the pan on a wire rack.

Serves 15

1 (2-layer) package chocolate cake mix
1 package chocolate instant pudding mix
1 cup (6 ounces) chocolate chips
4 eggs
1/4 cup vegetable oil
1 1/2 cups water

OATMEAL CHOCOLATE CHIP CAKE

1 3/4 cups boiling water
1 cup rolled oats
1/2 cup (1 stick) margarine, softened
1 cup granulated sugar
1 cup lightly packed brown sugar
2 extra-large eggs
1 3/4 cups all-purpose flour
1 tablespoon baking cocoa
1 teaspoon baking soda
1/2 teaspoon salt
2 cups (12 ounces) chocolate chips
3/4 cup walnuts

Pour the boiling water over the oats in a bowl and let stand for 10 minutes. Add the margarine, granulated sugar and brown sugar and beat until smooth. Beat in the eggs. Add the flour, baking cocoa, baking soda and salt and mix well. Stir in half the chocolate chips.

Spoon the batter into a greased and floured 9×13-inch cake pan. Sprinkle the walnuts and remaining chocolate chips over the top. Bake in a preheated 350-degree oven for 40 minutes. Cool in the pan on a wire rack.

Serves 15

CHOCOLATE CHIP ZUCCHINI CAKE

1/2 cup milk
1 1/2 teaspoons lemon juice
    or vinegar
2 1/2 cups all-purpose flour
1/4 cup baking cocoa
1/2 teaspoon baking powder
1 teaspoon baking soda
1/2 teaspoon ground cinnamon
1/2 teaspoon ground cloves
1/2 cup (1 stick) butter, softened
1/2 cup vegetable oil
1 3/4 cups sugar
2 eggs
1 teaspoon vanilla extract
2 cups seeded and finely
    chopped zucchini
1/2 cup (3 ounces) miniature
    chocolate chips

Combine the milk with the lemon juice in a measuring cup and stir to mix well. Let stand for 10 minutes to sour the milk. Mix the flour, baking cocoa, baking powder, baking soda, cinnamon and cloves together.

Combine the butter, oil and sugar in a mixing bowl and beat until creamy. Beat in the eggs, sour milk and vanilla. Add the dry ingredients and beat until smooth. Stir in the zucchini.

Spoon the batter into a greased 9×13-inch cake pan. Sprinkle with the chocolate chips. Bake in a preheated 325-degree oven for 40 to 45 minutes or until the cake tests done. Cool in the pan on a wire rack.

Serves 20

FROSTED CHOCOLATE CAKE

Cake

Mix the flour, sugar, baking cocoa, baking soda and salt in a large mixing bowl. Add the eggs, buttermilk and vanilla and beat just until smooth. Add the margarine and mix well.

Spoon the batter into a 9×13-inch cake pan sprayed with nonstick cooking spray. Bake in a preheated 325-degree oven for 45 minutes or until a wooden pick inserted near the center comes out clean. Cool in the pan on a wire rack for 10 minutes.

Frosting

Melt the margarine in a small saucepan; remove from the heat. Stir in the baking cocoa and milk. Add enough confectioners' sugar to make a thin frosting. Pour the frosting over the warm cake. Let stand until completely cool.

You can also prepare this in muffin cups or a larger glass baking dish, if desired. The cake freezes well.

Serves 12

Cake

2 cups all-purpose flour
2 cups sugar
4 tablespoons (heaping)
    baking cocoa
2 teaspoons (scant) baking soda
Pinch of salt
2 eggs
2 cups buttermilk, sour cream or
    light sour cream
1 teaspoon vanilla extract
1/2 cup (1 stick) margarine, melted

Confectioners' Sugar Frosting

2 tablespoons (rounded) margarine
4 tablespoons (heaping)
    baking cocoa
1/4 cup milk or hot water
Confectioners' sugar

Delegation from Indian region arriving at the Hundred Percent Club convention in Manila, Philippines, in 1967.

cakes 37

CHOCOLATE CINNAMON SNACKING CAKE

1/3 cup baking cocoa
1/2 teaspoon ground cinnamon
1/2 cup hot brewed coffee
3 eggs
2 cups sugar
1 cup mayonnaise or light
    mayonnaise
1 teaspoon vanilla extract
2 cups all-purpose flour
11/2 teaspoons baking soda
2/3 cup (4 ounces) miniature
    chocolate chips
Ground cinnamon
Confectioners' sugar

Mix the baking cocoa and 1/2 teaspoon cinnamon in a small heatproof bowl. Whisk in the hot coffee, blending well. Combine the eggs, sugar, mayonnaise and vanilla in a large bowl and whisk until smooth. Add the coffee mixture, flour and baking soda and whisk to mix well. Stir in the chocolate chips.

Coat a 9×13-inch cake pan with unsalted butter. Line the pan with waxed paper and butter the paper. Spoon the batter into the prepared pan. Bake in a preheated 350-degree oven for 40 minutes or until a wooden pick inserted near the center comes out clean. Cool in the pan for 10 minutes and invert onto a wire rack to cool for 1 hour.

Sprinkle the cake with additional cinnamon and confectioners' sugar. Cut into triangles and serve with lightly sweetened whipped cream or vanilla ice cream.

Serves 12

EARTHQUAKE CAKE

2 cups coconut
2 cups chopped nuts
1 (2-layer) package German
    chocolate cake mix
1/2 cup (1 stick) butter, melted
1 (1-pound) package
    confectioners' sugar
8 ounces cream cheese, softened

Sprinkle the coconut and nuts evenly in a 9×13-inch cake pan sprayed with nonstick cooking spray. Prepare the cake mix using the package directions. Spoon into the prepared pan.

Combine the butter with the confectioners' sugar and cream cheese in a bowl; mix until smooth. Drop by spoonfuls over the cake batter.

Bake the cake using the package directions. The cake batter will rise up around the cream cheese mixture. Cool in the pan on a wire rack. Cut into squares and invert onto plates to serve.

Serves 15

Mrs. Thomas J. Watson, Sr., was a guest of honor at a tea, August 24, 1957, sponsored by the Committee of Women's Activities of the IBM Country Club at Sands Point, New York.

cakes 39

HOT FUDGE CHOCOLATE CAKE

Cake
1 (2-layer) package chocolate
    cake mix
1 package vanilla instant
    pudding mix
3 eggs
1/2 cup milk

Fudgy Topping
2 jars hot fudge ice cream topping
2 or 3 small jars walnuts in syrup
    (optional)
16 ounces whipped topping
2 milk chocolate bars, grated,
    for garnish

Cake
Prepare the cake mix using the oil listed on the package, the pudding mix, eggs and milk. Bake in a greased and floured 9×13-inch cake pan using the package directions.

Topping
Remove the lids from the jars of hot fudge topping 10 minutes before the cake is done. Microwave on High for 2 minutes or until the sauce is bubbly and pours easily. Punch holes at 1-inch intervals in the hot cake with the handle of a wooden spoon. Pour the fudge sauce evenly over the cake and smooth with the spoon. Spoon the walnuts over the cake, distributing evenly.

Cover the pan with a lid or foil and chill in the refrigerator for 8 hours or longer. Spread the whipped topping over the cake and garnish with the grated chocolate. The flavor improves if the cake is stored in the refrigerator for 2 days before serving.

Serves 15

HEAVENLY CAKE

Prepare and bake the cake mix using the package directions for a 9×13-inch cake pan. Punch holes in the warm cake with the handle of a wooden spoon.

Pour the condensed milk over the cake and let stand for several minutes. Spoon the caramel sauce and then the hot fudge sauce over the cake.

Spread the whipped topping over the top and shave a candy bar over the topping with a vegetable peeler. Chill in the refrigerator for 4 hours or longer.

Serves 15

1 (2-layer) package chocolate
    cake mix
1 (14-ounce) can sweetened
    condensed milk
1/2 jar caramel ice cream sauce
1/2 jar hot fudge ice cream sauce
8 ounces whipped topping
Chocolate candy bar

Each year IBM recognizes the sales representatives who have achieved or exceeded their sales quota by inducting them into the Hundred Percent Club. The tradition began in 1925 when IBM president Thomas J. Watson, Sr., congratulated fifty-two qualifiers at IBM's first company-wide sales convention, held in Atlantic City, New Jersey. From 1933 to 1939, the Clubs met in New York City's Waldorf-Astoria Hotel. In 1940, the Club site was switched to Endicott, New York, where the qualifiers were housed in a sprawling "Tent City."

MISSISSIPPI MUD CAKE

Cake

1 cup (2 sticks) margarine, softened
2 cups sugar
1/2 cup baking cocoa
4 eggs
1/2 teaspoon salt
1 1/2 cups all-purpose flour
1 1/2 cups nuts
1 cup coconut
1 jar marshmallow creme

Mississippi Mud Frosting

1/2 cup (1 stick) margarine, softened
1/3 cup baking cocoa
1 teaspoon vanilla extract
1 (1-pound) package
    confectioners' sugar
4 to 5 tablespoons milk

Cake

Combine the margarine, sugar, baking cocoa, eggs and salt in a mixing bowl and mix until smooth. Add the flour, nuts and coconut; mix well.

Spoon the batter into a greased and floured 9×13-inch cake pan. Bake in a preheated 350-degree oven for 30 minutes. Spread the marshmallow creme over the hot cake. Cool in the pan on a wire rack.

Frosting

Cream the margarine with the baking cocoa and vanilla in a mixing bowl until light and fluffy. Add the confectioners' sugar and enough milk to make a smooth frosting, mixing well. Spread over the cake.

Serves 15

ONE-PAN PEANUT BUTTER CHOCOLATE CAKE

Combine the flour, sugar, baking cocoa, baking soda and salt in an ungreased 9×13-inch cake pan. Whisk until well mixed. Make three wells in the mixture. Pour the oil into the first well, the vinegar into the second well and the vanilla into the third well. Pour the water over the top and stir to mix well, scraping the sides and bottom of the pan. Wipe the edges of the pan.

Bake in a preheated 350-degree oven for 30 minutes or until a wooden pick inserted near the center comes out clean. Remove from the oven and turn off the oven. Sprinkle the cake with the peanut butter bites and return to the oven, leaving the oven door ajar. Let stand for 5 minutes. Remove from the oven and spread the melted bites evenly over the cake. Cool in the pan on a wire rack.

Serves 12 to 15

2 2/3 cups all-purpose flour
2 1/4 cups sugar
1 cup baking cocoa
2 teaspoons baking soda
1 teaspoon salt
3/4 cup vegetable oil
2 tablespoons white vinegar
1 tablespoon vanilla extract
2 cups lukewarm water
1 (12-ounce) package Reese's peanut butter bites, chocolate chips or York peppermint bites

SCREWBALL DARK CHOCOLATE CAKE

Combine the flour, sugar, baking cocoa, baking soda and salt in a 9×13-inch cake pan. Make three wells in the mixture. Pour the vinegar into the first well, the vanilla into the second well and the oil into the third well. Pour the water over the top.

Bake in a preheated 350-degree oven for 30 to 60 minutes or until a wooden pick inserted near the center comes out clean. Cool in the pan on a wire rack.

Serves 15

3 cups all-purpose flour
2 cups sugar
3/4 cup baking cocoa
2 teaspoons baking soda
1 teaspoon salt
2 teaspoons vinegar
2 teaspoons vanilla extract
1 cup vegetable oil
2 cups cold water

cakes 43

WACKY CAKE

Cake

3 cups all-purpose flour
2 cups sugar
1/3 cup baking cocoa
2 teaspoons baking soda
1 teaspoon salt
1 teaspoon vanilla extract
1 tablespoon vinegar
6 tablespoons vegetable oil
2 cups water

Wacky Frosting

2 1/3 cups confectioners' sugar
1/4 cup baking cocoa (optional)
1/4 cup (1/2 stick) margarine,
    softened
1/2 teaspoon vanilla extract
1 to 3 tablespoons water

Cake

Sift the flour, sugar, baking cocoa, baking soda and salt into a greased 9×13-inch cake pan. Make three wells in the mixture. Pour the vanilla into one well, the vinegar into the second well and the oil into the third well. Pour the water over the top and stir with a fork just until moistened.

Bake in a preheated 350-degree oven for 35 to 45 minutes or until a knife inserted near the center comes out clean. Cool in the pan on a wire rack.

Frosting

Mix the confectioners' sugar and baking cocoa in a mixing bowl. Add the margarine, vanilla and 1 tablespoon of the water. Mix at low speed, adding additional water and mixing to the desired consistency. Spread over the cake.

This cake is egg-free, milk-free and nut-free. It was popular during World War II, when there were shortages, and is good now for people with allergies. You can also prepare the cake by placing 2 eggs in the first well and combining the vinegar and vanilla in one well. Reduce the 2 cups water to 1 1/2 cups hot water, taking care not to pour the water directly onto the eggs before mixing.

Serves 12

Cowboy boots and ten-gallon hats help Arizona IBMers welcome the IBM Texas delegation to the 1955 Hundred Percent Club Convention in Los Angeles, California.

NAVY CAKE

2 cups all-purpose flour
2 cups sugar
1/2 cup baking cocoa
2 1/2 teaspoons baking soda
1 teaspoon salt
2 eggs
1 cup vegetable oil
1 cup buttermilk
1 cup hot water
1 teaspoon vanilla extract

Sift the flour, sugar, baking cocoa, baking soda and salt together. Combine the eggs, oil, buttermilk, water and vanilla in a mixing bowl and mix well. Add the dry ingredients and mix until smooth.

Spoon into an ungreased 9×13-inch cake pan. Bake in a preheated 350-degree oven for 45 minutes. Cool in the pan on a wire rack. Frost as desired or dust with confectioners' sugar.

Serves 18

CHOCOLATE SYRUP CAKE

1/2 cup (1 stick) butter, softened
1 cup sugar
4 eggs, beaten
1 cup all-purpose flour
1 teaspoon baking powder
1/2 teaspoon salt
1 (16-ounce) can chocolate syrup
1 teaspoon vanilla extract

Cream the butter and sugar in a mixing bowl until light and fluffy. Beat in the eggs. Add the flour, baking powder and salt and mix well. Stir in the chocolate syrup and vanilla; the batter will be thin.

Spoon the batter into a greased 9×13-inch cake pan. Bake in a preheated 350-degree oven for 25 to 30 minutes or until a wooden pick inserted near the center comes out clean. Frost with a classic buttercream frosting or fudge frosting, if desired. You can double the recipe for a larger layer cake.

Serves 15

TRIPLE CHOCOLATE CAKE

Combine the cake mix, pudding mix, chocolate chips, milk and eggs in a large bowl. Mix by hand for 2 minutes or until combined.

Spoon the batter into a greased and floured 9×13-inch cake pan. Bake in a preheated 350-degree oven for 50 to 55 minutes or until a wooden pick inserted near the center comes out clean. Cool in the pan on a wire rack. Top each serving with a dollop of whipped cream.

Serves 12

1 (2-layer) package chocolate
   cake mix
1 package chocolate instant
   pudding mix
2 cups (12 ounces) chocolate chips
1 3/4 cups milk
2 eggs
Whipped cream to taste

CHOCOLATE SHEET CAKE

Cake
Combine the baking cocoa, margarine and water in a saucepan. Bring to a boil, stirring to blend well. Remove from the heat.

Mix the flour, sugar, baking soda and salt in a large bowl. Blend the milk and vinegar in a small bowl. Add to the dry ingredients and mix well. Beat in the eggs. Add the chocolate mixture and vanilla and beat for 1 minute longer.

Spray a 13×20-inch baking sheet with a 1-inch rim with nonstick baking spray. Spoon the batter into the prepared baking sheet. Bake in a preheated 350-degree oven for 15 to 20 minutes or until the cake tests done.

Frosting
Combine the baking cocoa, margarine and milk in a saucepan. Bring to a boil, stirring to blend well. Remove from the heat and add enough confectioners' sugar to make a frosting of spreading consistency. Pour the hot frosting over the hot cake and sprinkle with the walnuts. Cool in the pan on a wire rack.

Serves 24

Cake
3 1/2 tablespoons baking cocoa
1 cup (2 sticks) margarine
1 cup water
2 cups all-purpose flour
2 cups sugar
1 teaspoon baking soda
1/4 teaspoon salt
1/2 cup milk
1 tablespoon vinegar
2 eggs
1 teaspoon vanilla extract

Sheet Cake Frosting
3 1/2 tablespoons baking cocoa
1/2 cup (1 stick) margarine
6 tablespoons milk
2 cups (or more)
   confectioners' sugar
1/2 cup chopped walnuts

Tom Laster with Thomas J. Watson, Sr., at the 1948 Hundred Percent Club held in Endicott, New York, 1949.

TEXAS SHEET CAKE

Cake

Mix the flour, sugar and salt together in a large bowl. Combine the margarine, baking cocoa and water in a saucepan. Bring to a boil, stirring to blend well. Remove from the heat. Add to the flour mixture. Beat the eggs with the sour cream and baking soda in a small bowl. Add to the batter and mix well.

Spoon the batter into a greased and floured rimmed 11×15-inch baking sheet. Bake in a preheated 350-degree oven for 15 to 20 minutes or until a wooden pick inserted near the center comes out clean.

Frosting

Melt the margarine in the same saucepan used to heat the chocolate mixture for the cake; do not boil. Stir in the baking cocoa. Remove from the heat and pour into a mixing bowl. Stir in the vanilla. Add the confectioners' sugar alternately with enough evaporated milk to make a frosting of spreading consistency. Spread the frosting over the hot cake and sprinkle with the pecans. Cool in the pan on a wire rack.

Serves 30

Cake

2 cups all-purpose flour
2 cups sugar
1/2 teaspoon salt
1 cup (2 sticks) margarine
1/4 cup baking cocoa
1 cup water
2 eggs
1 cup sour cream or buttermilk
1 teaspoon baking soda

Texas Sheet Cake Frosting

1/2 cup (1 stick) margarine
1/4 cup baking cocoa
1 teaspoon vanilla extract
1 (1-pound) package
    confectioners' sugar
5 to 6 tablespoons evaporated milk,
    whole milk or heavy cream
1 cup chopped pecans or walnuts
    (optional)

AMAZINGLY RICH INDIVIDUAL CHOCOLATE PUDDING CAKES

Rich Topping

5 tablespoons granulated sugar
5 tablespoons light brown sugar
1/2 cup Dutch-process baking cocoa

Cakes

1 cup all-purpose flour
2 tablespoons Dutch-process
    baking cocoa
1 1/2 teaspoons baking powder
1/4 teaspoon ground cinnamon
1/2 teaspoon salt
2 tablespoons unsalted butter,
    softened
2/3 cup sugar
1/2 teaspoon vanilla extract
1/2 cup milk
1 (2-ounce) toffee bar or white
    chocolate bar, chopped
1 1/2 cups boiling water

Topping

Combine the granulated sugar and brown sugar in a small bowl, mixing to blend well. Sift in the baking cocoa and mix well.

Cakes

Sift the flour, baking cocoa, baking powder, cinnamon and salt into a medium bowl. Cream the butter with the sugar and vanilla in a mixing bowl until light and fluffy. Add the dry ingredients and milk; mix well. Stir in the toffee bits.

Place six ramekins 3 1/2 inches in diameter and 1 1/2 inches deep on a baking sheet. Spoon the batter evenly into the ramekins and sprinkle with the topping. Add 1/4 cup of the boiling water to each ramekin. Bake in a preheated 350-degree oven for 25 to 28 minutes or until set. Serve immediately topped with vanilla ice cream.

Serves 6

CHOCOLATE LAVA CAKES
(MOELLEUX AU CHOCOLAT)

Melt the chocolate in a double boiler over simmering water. Remove from the heat and add the butter, mixing to blend well. Beat the eggs with the sugar in a mixing bowl until pale yellow. Stir in the chocolate mixture and the flour.

Spoon into four buttered ramekins. Place on a baking sheet. Bake in a preheated 350-degree oven for 10 minutes or until the cakes are set but the center is still liquid. Invert onto dessert plates to serve. Serve with vanilla ice cream or raspberry sauce.

Serves 4

6 ounces semisweet chocolate or 70% dark chocolate
$3/4$ cup ($1^1/2$ sticks) butter, chopped and softened
3 eggs
$1/2$ cup sugar
$1/3$ cup all-purpose flour

CHOCOLATE CHERRY CUPCAKES

Combine the cake mix, pie filling, eggs and baking cocoa in a mixing bowl and beat for 2 minutes. Grease and flour twenty-four muffin cups or spray with nonstick cooking spray. Spoon the batter into the prepared muffin cups.

Bake in a preheated 350-degree oven for 15 to 20 minutes or until the cupcakes test done. Cool in the pan on a wire rack and frost as desired.

You can also prepare this in a 9×13-inch baking pan and bake for 25 to 30 minutes, if preferred.

Serves 24

1 (2-layer) package devil's food cake mix
1 (16-ounce) can cherry pie filling
3 eggs
$1/4$ cup baking cocoa

MACAROON-FILLED
CHOCOLATE CUPCAKES

Coconut Filling
1 cup fat-free ricotta cheese
1/4 cup sugar
1 egg white
1/3 cup flaked coconut
1 teaspoon coconut extract

Cupcakes
11/4 cups all-purpose flour
1 cup sugar
1/3 cup baking cocoa
11/2 teaspoons baking soda
2 egg whites
3/4 cup buttermilk
1/3 cup unsweetened applesauce
1 teaspoon vanilla extract

Filling
Combine the ricotta cheese, sugar, egg white, coconut and coconut extract in a small bowl and mix well.

Cupcakes
Mix the flour, sugar, baking cocoa and baking soda in a medium bowl. Add the egg whites, buttermilk, applesauce and vanilla; mix until smooth.

Spray twelve muffin cups with nonstick cooking spray or line with paper liners. Spoon half the cupcake batter into the prepared muffin cups. Spoon a rounded teaspoon of the filling into each cup and top with the remaining cupcake batter, filling 3/4 full. Bake in a preheated 350-degree oven for 25 minutes. Cool in the pan on a wire rack.

Serves 12

*IBM World Trade Corporation 1956 Hundred Percent Club Convention
held in Canada at the Manoir Saint Castin Hotel.*

SURPRISE CUPCAKES

1 (2-layer) package German
    chocolate cake mix
8 ounces cream cheese, softened
1/3 cup sugar
1 egg
Pinch of salt
1 cup (6 ounces) chocolate chips

Prepare the cake mix using the package directions. Spoon the batter into twenty-two paper-lined muffin cups, filling 1/2 to 2/3 full.

Combine the cream cheese and sugar in a mixing bowl and beat until light and fluffy. Beat in the egg and salt. Stir in the chocolate chips. Drop by rounded teaspoonfuls onto the cupcake batter. Bake using the directions on the cake mix package. Cool in the pan on a wire rack.

Makes 22 cupcakes

FUDGE FROSTING

1 (1-pound) package
    confectioners' sugar, sifted
1/2 cup baking cocoa
1/4 teaspoon salt
1/3 cup boiling water
1/3 cup butter, softened
1 teaspoon vanilla extract

Combine the confectioners' sugar, baking cocoa and salt in a mixing bowl. Add the water and butter; mix until smooth. Mix in the vanilla.

Frosts 1 cake

CHOCOLATE PEANUT BUTTER FROSTING

Combine the chocolate syrup and chocolate in a small saucepan.
Heat over low heat until the chocolate melts, stirring to blend well.
Combine with the peanut butter in a large bowl and mix well.
Add the confectioners' sugar and then the milk, stirring until smooth.

Frosts 1 cake

3/4 cup chocolate syrup
8 ounces semisweet chocolate,
  chopped
2 cups creamy peanut butter
1 cup confectioners' sugar
1/4 cup milk

*Cake baked for the Fortieth
Anniversary tribute to Thomas J.
Watson, Sr.*

candies

Dayton Coffee Grinder customer, Rio de Janeiro, Brazil, May 4, 1933.

PRODUCTS

From its modest beginning manufacturing punch card machines,

grocery scales, cheese slicers, and time clocks to its emergence as

one of the world's largest companies, IBM has always been in

the process of transforming itself to meet the needs of its clients, lead

the industry, and change the world. The black-and-white photographs

of men and women in factories and branch offices in the early

twentieth century and the colorful

magnified views of microelectronics from

just a few years ago all show an IBM that

is very much in motion.

BRIGADEIRO 60

CHOCOLATE CLUSTERS 60

CORDIAL CHERRIES 61

CHOCOLATE FLICK 61

CHOCOLATE FUDGE 62

CHOCOLATE CHEESE FUDGE 62

FANTASY FUDGE 64

FOOLPROOF FUDGE 64

LAYERED MINT FUDGE 66

ROCKY ROAD FUDGE 66

SNICKERS FUDGE 67

MILLIONAIRE CANDY 69

TEXAS MILLIONAIRES 70

PEANUT BUTTER CHEWS 71

PEANUT BUTTER BONBONS 72

CHOCOLATE PIZZA 73

BEST-EVER ENGLISH TOFFEE 74

GERMAN CHOCOLATE RUM
CLUSTERS 74

CHOCOLATE RASPBERRY
TRUFFLES 76

OREO TRUFFLES 77

CHOCOLATE TRUFFLES 77

TRUFFLES WITH A TWIST 79

CHOCOLATE PEANUT
BUTTER TRUFFLES 80

WHITE CHOCOLATE
AVOCADO TRUFFLES 80

BRIGADEIRO

1 (14-ounce) can sweetened
    condensed milk
2 tablespoons unsalted butter
3 tablespoons baking cocoa
Granulated chocolate or
    chocolate jimmies

Combine the condensed milk, butter and baking cocoa in a saucepan. Cook over medium-low heat, stirring constantly, until the mixture thickens enough that the spoon leaves a clear path on the bottom of the saucepan. Pour into a greased dish and cool to room temperature or chill in the refrigerator.

Shape the cooled mixture into 1 1/2-inch balls with hands coated with butter. Roll in granulated chocolate to coat evenly.

You can cook the mixture for 5 minutes longer if the balls do not hold their shape. This is a traditional party food in Brazil.

Makes 40 balls

CHOCOLATE CLUSTERS

1 cup (6 ounces) semisweet
    chocolate chips
1/2 cup (1 stick) butter
16 large marshmallows
1/2 teaspoon vanilla extract
1 cup flaked coconut
2 cups rolled oats

Combine the chocolate chips, butter and marshmallows in a large saucepan. Cook over low heat until the ingredients melt, stirring to blend well. Remove from the heat and stir in the vanilla.

Add the coconut and oats to the chocolate mixture and mix well. Drop by teaspoonfuls onto waxed paper. Chill in the refrigerator until firm.

Makes 42 clusters

CORDIAL CHERRIES

Drain the cherries, discarding the liquid. Return the cherries to the jar and add the brandy. Cover and freeze for 8 hours. Drain the cherries, reserving the brandy for another use; pat the cherries dry with a paper towel.

Melt the chocolate in a small saucepan using the package directions. Dip each cherry quickly into the melted chocolate, coating evenly. Place stem side up on waxed paper. Let stand until the chocolate is cool and set.

Serves 12

1 (10-ounce) jar maraschino cherries
1/2 cup brandy
8 ounces bittersweet chocolate

CHOCOLATE FLICK

Combine the chocolate chips and peanut butter in a microwave-safe 2-quart bowl. Microwave on Medium for 5 minutes or until melted; stir to mix well. Fold in the marshmallows.

Spoon the mixture into an 8×8-inch foil pan and smooth evenly. Freeze until firm. Cut into squares and store in a plastic bag until serving time.

Serves 10

2 cups (12 ounces) chocolate chips
1 cup chunky peanut butter
3 cups miniature marshmallows

CHOCOLATE FUDGE

1/2 cup (1 stick) butter
4 1/2 cups sugar
1 (12-ounce) can evaporated milk
8 ounces marshmallows
2 ounces unsweetened
    baking chocolate
2 cups (12 ounces) semisweet
    chocolate chips
12 ounces German's
    sweet chocolate
2 cups chopped nuts
1 tablespoon vanilla extract

Combine the butter, sugar and evaporated milk in a large saucepan. Heat over medium heat until the butter melts and the sugar dissolves, stirring to blend well. Bring to a boil and boil for 5 minutes. Add the marshmallows and cook until melted, stirring constantly.

Add the baking chocolate, chocolate chips and German's chocolate in the order listed, cooking until the chocolate melts after each addition and stirring constantly to mix well. Stir in the nuts and vanilla. Pour into a 10×15-inch pan and let stand until cool. Cut into squares.

Makes 5 pounds

CHOCOLATE CHEESE FUDGE

8 ounces Velveeta cheese, sliced
1 cup (2 sticks) butter
1 cup chopped pecans or walnuts
    (optional)
1 teaspoon vanilla extract
2 (1-pound) packages
    confectioners' sugar
1/2 cup baking cocoa

Combine the cheese and butter in a saucepan. Melt over medium heat, stirring constantly to blend well. Remove from the heat and stir in the pecans and vanilla.

Sift the confectioners' sugar and baking cocoa into a large bowl. Add the melted cheese mixture and mix well; the mixture will be very stiff.

Spray the bottom of a 9×9-inch pan lightly with nonstick cooking spray. Press the fudge evenly and firmly into the pan. Pat the surface with a paper towel to remove the excess oil. Chill until firm and cut into squares.

Makes 36 squares

This 1925 photograph features a Morris Commercial one-ton van used by
International Business Machines Co., Ltd., in London to deliver various Dayton Scale Company
products, such as coffee mills, bread slicers, meat choppers, and bacon slicers.

FANTASY FUDGE

3 cups sugar
3/4 cup (1 1/2 sticks) butter
    or margarine
1 (5-ounce) can evaporated milk
2 cups (12 ounces) semisweet
    chocolate chips
1 (7-ounce) jar marshmallow creme
1 cup chopped nuts
1 teaspoon vanilla extract

Combine the sugar, butter and evaporated milk in a heavy 2- to 3-quart saucepan. Bring to a full rolling boil, stirring constantly. Boil over medium heat for 5 minutes or to 234 degrees on a candy thermometer, soft-ball stage, stirring constantly.

Remove from the heat and stir in the chocolate chips until melted. Add the marshmallow creme, nuts and vanilla; mix well. Spread in a greased 9×13-inch dish and cool to room temperature. Cut into squares.

Makes 3 pounds

FOOLPROOF FUDGE

2 2/3 cups (16 ounces) semisweet
    chocolate chips
1 (14-ounce) can sweetened
    condensed milk
2/3 cup walnuts or pecans, or
    2 cups miniature marshmallows
2 teaspoons vanilla extract

Combine the chocolate chips and condensed milk in a heavy saucepan. Heat over low heat until the chocolate chips melt, stirring constantly to blend well. Remove from the heat and let stand for 1 minute. Stir in the walnuts and vanilla.

Spoon into an 8×8-inch pan lined with foil or waxed paper. Chill for 3 hours or until firm. Invert onto a platter and remove the foil. Cut into 1-inch squares.

Makes 64 squares

MORE MONEY
...*in* CANDY

A Dayton Moneyweight Candy Scale, introduced in the early 1900s and manufactured by the Dayton Scale Company, which was a division of IBM.

LAYERED MINT FUDGE

1 (14-ounce) can sweetened
    condensed milk
2 cups (12 ounces) semisweet
    chocolate chips
2 teaspoons vanilla extract
1 cup (6 ounces) white
    chocolate chips
1 tablespoon peppermint extract
1 or 2 drops of green food coloring

Line a 9×9-inch pan with foil and butter the foil. Combine 1 cup of the condensed milk with the semisweet chocolate chips in a microwave-safe bowl. Microwave on High for 3 minutes, stirring after 1 1/2 minutes. Stir in the vanilla. Spoon half the mixture into the prepared pan. Chill until set.

Combine the remaining condensed milk with the white chocolate chips in a microwave-safe bowl. Microwave on High for 2 minutes, stirring after 1 minute. Stir in the peppermint extract and the food coloring. Spread over the chilled layer. Chill until set.

Reheat the remaining semisweet chocolate mixture and spread over the mint layer. Chill for 8 hours or until set. Cut into 1-inch squares.

Makes 81 squares

ROCKY ROAD FUDGE

2 cups (12 ounces) semisweet
    chocolate chips
1 cup (6 ounces) butterscotch chips
1 cup chunky peanut butter
1 tablespoon butter or margarine
1 (10-ounce) package miniature
    marshmallows

Grease a 9×9-inch metal pan and line with plastic wrap. Combine the chocolate chips, butterscotch chips, peanut butter and butter in a 4-quart saucepan. Cook over medium heat for 2 to 3 minutes or until the ingredients melt, stirring constantly to blend. Remove from the heat and stir in the marshmallows.

Spread evenly in the prepared pan. Cover with plastic wrap and chill for 3 hours or until firm. Invert onto a cutting board and remove the plastic wrap. Invert the fudge again and cut into 36 squares. Store in the refrigerator.

Makes 36 squares

SNICKERS FUDGE

Combine the chocolate chips, butterscotch chips and 1 1/2 cup peanut butter in a microwave-safe bowl. Microwave on High for 2 minutes, stirring after 1 minute. Spread half the mixture evenly in a 9×13-inch pan. Chill until firm.

Melt the butter in a heavy saucepan. Stir in the sugar and evaporated milk. Bring to a boil and boil for 5 minutes. Remove from the heat and stir in the marshmallow creme. Stir in 1/4 cup peanut butter, the peanuts and vanilla. Spread over the chilled layer and chill until firm.

Combine the caramels with the cream in a microwave-safe bowl. Microwave on High until the caramels melt, stirring to blend well. Spread over the peanut layer and chill until firm.

Microwave the remaining chocolate chip mixture just enough to reheat to spreading consistency. Spread over the caramel layer. Chill for 8 hours or until firm. Cut into 1-inch squares.

Makes 117 squares

2 cups (12 ounces) semisweet
    chocolate chips
1/2 cup (3 ounces)
    butterscotch chips
1/2 cup peanut butter
1/4 cup (1/2 stick) butter
    or margarine
1 cup sugar
1/4 cup evaporated milk
1 (7-ounce) jar marshmallow creme
1/4 cup peanut butter
1 1/2 cups salted peanuts, chopped
1 teaspoon vanilla extract
1 (14-ounce) package
    caramel candies
1/4 cup whipping cream

Employees punching in on IBM's International Dial Recorders at the entrance to the Wireless Department of A. J. Stevens & Co., Ltd., Wolverhampton, England, in 1926.

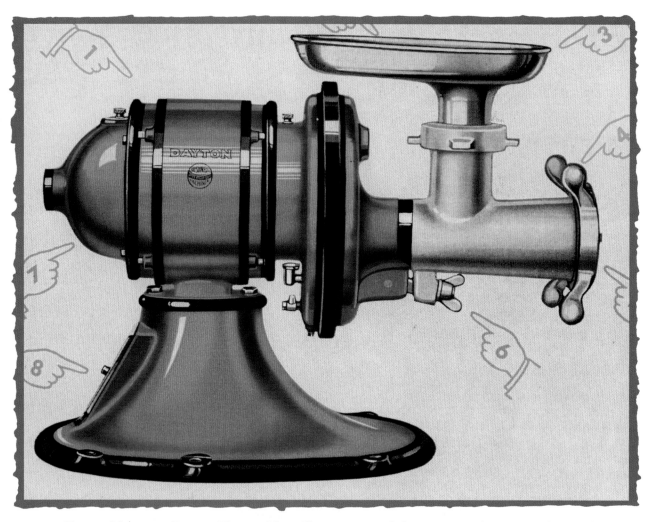

Pictured here is a Dayton Electric Meat Chopper, one of the many products manufactured by the Dayton Scale Company division of IBM in the early 1900s.

MILLIONAIRE CANDY

Combine the brown sugar, granulated sugar, corn syrup, butter and 1 cup of the evaporated milk in a saucepan. Bring to a boil, stirring constantly. Add the remaining 1 cup evaporated milk gradually, maintaining the mixture at a boil. Stir in the pecans and vanilla.

Cook the mixture to 234 to 240 degrees on a candy thermometer, soft-ball stage. Pour into a buttered 9×13-inch pan. Chill in the refrigerator for 8 hours or longer. Cut into small squares.

Melt the chocolate chips with a small amount of paraffin in a double boiler, stirring to blend well. Dip the candy squares into the chocolate, coating evenly. Place on waxed paper to cool.

Makes about 100 squares

1 cup packed brown sugar
1 cup granulated sugar
1 cup light corn syrup
1 cup (2 sticks) butter
2 cups evaporated milk
1 pound pecans
1 tablespoon vanilla extract
2 cups (12 ounces) chocolate chips
Paraffin

TEXAS MILLIONAIRES

1 (14-ounce) package
    caramel candies
2 tablespoons butter or margarine
2 tablespoons water
3 cups pecan halves
1 cup (6 ounces) semisweet
    chocolate chips
2 ounces vanilla candy coating or
    almond bark coating

Combine the caramel candies, butter and water in a heavy saucepan. Heat over low heat until the candies and butter melt, stirring to blend well. Stir in the pecan halves. Cool in the saucepan for 5 minutes. Drop by tablespoonfuls onto lightly greased waxed paper. Chill in the refrigerator for 1 hour or in the freezer for 20 minutes.

Melt the chocolate chips and candy coating in a heavy saucepan over low heat, stirring until smooth. Dip the candies into the chocolate mixture, allowing the excess to drip back into the saucepan. Place on lightly greased waxed paper. Let stand until firm. Chill in the refrigerator for 1 hour or in the freezer for 20 minutes.

Makes 4 dozen

Since their plant in Woodbridge, New Jersey, took up four square miles, the people at Curtiss-Wright Corporation wanted to make it easier for IBM Customer Engineer Stanley Sorenson to check out all the IBM typewriters in the place. Their solution: a specifically built tricycle for him to use in making his rounds.

PEANUT BUTTER CHEWS

Combine 1 cup peanut butter and 8 ounces baking chocolate with the corn syrup and water in a double boiler. Heat over simmering water until the chocolate melts, stirring to blend well. Remove from the heat and stir in the peanuts and cereal. Spread on a lightly buttered 10×15-inch rimmed nonstick baking sheet.

Melt the white chocolate with 1 1/4 cups peanut butter in a double boiler over simmering water, stirring to mix well. Spread over the semisweet chocolate layer.

Melt 2 ounces baking chocolate in a double boiler over simmering heat. Drizzle over the layers. Draw a knife through the topping to decorate, if desired. Chill in the refrigerator until firm. Cut with a cookie cutter or cut into small diagonal pieces. Serve in miniature paper cups, if desired.

Makes 4 dozen

1 cup creamy peanut butter
8 ounces semisweet
    baking chocolate
1 cup light corn syrup
1 tablespoon water
2 cups unsalted peanuts, crushed
4 cups crisp rice cereal
12 ounces white chocolate
1 1/4 cups creamy peanut butter
2 ounces semisweet
    baking chocolate

PEANUT BUTTER BONBONS

3 cups crisp rice cereal
2 cups confectioners' sugar
1/2 cup (1 stick) butter
2 cups creamy peanut butter
2 to 2 1/2 cups (12 to 15 ounces)
    semisweet chocolate chips or
    milk chocolate chips
1/3 bar paraffin

Toss the cereal with the confectioners' sugar in a large bowl. Melt the butter with the peanut butter in a saucepan, stirring to blend well. Pour over the cereal mixture and stir to combine. Chill in the refrigerator.

Shape into 1/2-inch balls and place on a waxed paper-lined baking sheet, adding additional confectioners' sugar while shaping if needed to reduce stickiness. Chill in the refrigerator for 1 hour.

Melt the chocolate chips with the paraffin in a double boiler over simmering water, stirring to mix well. Dip the bonbons into the chocolate mixture and return to the baking sheet. Store in the refrigerator.

Makes 100 bonbons

CHOCOLATE PIZZA

Combine the chocolate chips and 14 ounces almond bark in a 2-quart microwave-safe bowl. Microwave on High for 2 minutes and stir. Microwave for 1 to 2 minutes longer or until smooth, stirring every 30 seconds. Stir in the marshmallows, cereal and peanuts. Spread in a greased 12-inch pizza pan. Top with the red and green cherries and sprinkle with the coconut.

Combine 2 ounces almond bark with the oil in a 1-cup microwave-safe measuring cup. Microwave on High for 1 minute and stir. Microwave for 30 to 60 seconds longer or until smooth, stirring every 15 seconds. Drizzle over the pizza. Chill until firm. Store at room temperature. Cut into wedges to serve.

Serves 8 to 12

2 cups (12 ounces) semisweet
   chocolate chips
14 ounces white almond bark
2 cups miniature marshmallows
1 cup crisp rice cereal
1 cup peanuts
1 (16-ounce) jar red maraschino
   cherries, drained and cut
   into halves
1/4 cup drained and quartered
   green maraschino cherries
1/2 cup flaked coconut
2 ounces white almond bark
1 teaspoon vegetable oil

Announced on September 27, 1946, the IBM 603 Electronic Multiplier was the first electronic calculator ever placed into production.
It consisted of two boxes: the Type 603 calculating unit and Type 520 punch-read unit.

BEST-EVER ENGLISH TOFFEE

1/3 cup slivered almonds
1 cup (2 sticks) butter
1 cup sugar
3 milk chocolate bars, broken
   into pieces
1/2 cup finely chopped walnuts

Sprinkle the almonds evenly in a 10×15-inch pan sprayed with nonstick cooking spray. Combine the butter and sugar in a medium saucepan without a nonstick surface. Cook over medium-high heat for 5 to 7 minutes or until the mixture is a golden caramel color. Spread evenly over the almonds in the prepared pan.

Sprinkle the chocolate over the caramel mixture immediately and spread evenly with a spatula as it melts. Sprinkle the walnuts over the top and press lightly into the chocolate. Chill in the refrigerator until set. Break into pieces and store in the refrigerator. Let stand at room temperature for 5 minutes before serving.

Serves 10

GERMAN CHOCOLATE RUM CLUSTERS

1 block palmin, melted and cooled
1 cup baking cocoa
1 tablespoon rum
1 (1-pound) package
   confectioners' sugar
Chopped nuts

Combine the palmin, baking cocoa and rum in a bowl. Add the confectioners' sugar gradually, mixing well after each addition. Stir in nuts. Drop by spoonfuls onto waxed paper. Store in the refrigerator.

Palmin is coconut fat and can be found in a German deli.

Makes 2 dozen clusters

No ... the IBM Electric <u>can't</u> handle the petty cash but ...

it will produce

better typing ...

save time

and money, too!

The IBM gives you typing to be proud of—always uniform no matter what touch a typist uses. And it's the world's *simplest* electric in design and operation, the most *dependable* in performance.

The IBM saves money, too, because it helps turn out more typing in less time—helps handle more business without added secretarial expense.

And remember, IBM is the world leader in electric typewriter progress—the only electric available with proportional spacing and *electronic* tabulating.

IBM ELECTRIC TYPEWRITERS

The IBM Electric is available in these 7 handsome colors

Here's the newest IBM color—exciting Titian Glow

—OUTSELL ALL OTHER ELECTRICS COMBINED!

Print ad for the IBM electric typewriter, 1957.

CHOCOLATE RASPBERRY TRUFFLES

1¹/2 cups heavy cream
16 ounces semisweet
    chocolate, chopped
¹/2 cup raspberry purée
Pinch of salt
1 cup Dutch-process baking cocoa

Heat the cream just to a boil in a small saucepan. Pour immediately over the chocolate in a medium heatproof bowl; stir to melt the chocolate and blend well. Stir in the raspberry purée and salt. Chill in the refrigerator for 1 hour.

Scoop the mixture into 1-inch balls with a melon scooper. Roll in the baking cocoa in a bowl, coating well. Store in the refrigerator until serving time.

Makes 60 truffles

Making a perfect impression, Miss Marilyn Brown demonstrates an IBM Electric Typewriter at the Office Management Association of Chicago's Thirteenth Annual Seminar and Business Show held in the spring of 1955. Miss Brown, with unspilled water beakers on her wrists, easily types 150 words a minute.

OREO TRUFFLES

Crush nine of the cookies in a food processor or place in a sealable plastic bag and crush with a rolling pin; reserve for later use. Crush the remaining cookies to fine crumbs in the same manner. Combine with the cream cheese in a medium bowl and mix well. Shape into forty-two 1-inch balls.

Melt the chocolate in a double boiler over simmering water, stirring until smooth. Dip the balls into the chocolate and place on a waxed paper-lined baking sheet. Sprinkle with the reserved cookie crumbs. Chill in the refrigerator for 1 hour or until firm. Store, covered, in the refrigerator.

The chocolate will be easier to work with if you melt it with a small amount of butter.

Makes 42 truffles

1 (16-ounce) package Oreo chocolate sandwich cookies or peanut butter cookies
8 ounces cream cheese, softened
2 2/3 cups (16 ounces) chopped semisweet baking chocolate, or semisweet chocolate chips

CHOCOLATE TRUFFLES

Melt the chocolate in a double boiler over simmering water. Remove from the heat and add the butter and egg yolk; mix well. Stir in the coffee extract. Let stand until cool and firm. Shape into balls and coat with baking cocoa. Store in the refrigerator.

If you are concerned about using raw egg yolks, use yolks from eggs pasteurized in their shells, which are sold at some specialty food stores, or use an equivalent amount of pasteurized egg substitute.

Serves 6

6 ounces bittersweet chocolate
2 tablespoons butter
1 egg yolk
1 teaspoon coffee extract
Baking cocoa

**The More It Costs to Do Business
The Less You Can Tolerate Waste**

ASCENDING operating costs call for increased accuracy, greater simplicity—**Complete and assured protection**—in all computing departments of the business world.

You get those necessary factors in the simplest, safest, most practical form through International Time and Cost Recorders, Tabulating Machines and Computing Scales.

Write us for full details on the kind of "International" efficiency which interests YOU

Computing-Tabulating-Recording Company

50 BROAD ST., NEW YORK, N. Y.

Nine years after it was formed in 1911, the Computing-Tabulating-Recording Company (CTR) published this ad illustrating some of its major offerings. Back then, the company (which was later renamed IBM in 1924) sold a variety of time equipment (seen at the top), including dial recorders and time stamps; tabulating equipment (at lower left), including vertical sorters and key punches; and scales (at lower right), including one- and two-arm fan scales.

TRUFFLES WITH A TWIST

Process the chocolate in a food processor until finely chopped. Combine the cream and espresso in a heavy medium saucepan. Bring just to a boil, whisking constantly to mix well. Remove from the heat and add the chocolate, stirring to melt and blend completely. Stir in the Kahlúa.

Spread the mixture in a shallow pan and chill in the refrigerator for 30 minutes. Stir in the crushed ginger beans. Cover with plastic wrap and chill for 2 hours or longer.

Spread the baking cocoa on a plate and coat hands with additional cocoa. Shape the chocolate mixture into balls and roll in the baking cocoa, coating evenly. Place on a serving plate. Store, covered, in the refrigerator for up to 1 week.

Makes 30 truffles

8 ounces bittersweet chocolate

1/2 cup plus 2 tablespoons heavy cream

2 1/2 tablespoons brewed espresso, or 1 1/2 teaspoons instant espresso granules

2 tablespoons Kahlúa

1/2 cup crushed dark chocolate-coated ginger beans, espresso beans, raisins or nuts

1/4 cup Dutch-process baking cocoa

candies 79

CHOCOLATE PEANUT BUTTER TRUFFLES

8 ounces semisweet chocolate
1/2 cup peanut butter
8 ounces whipped topping
Confectioners' sugar, chopped
    pecans, flaked coconut or
    baking cocoa

Microwave the chocolate in a large microwave-safe bowl for 2 minutes or until almost melted. Stir until smooth. Stir in the peanut butter. Let cool to room temperature.

Add the whipped topping to the peanut butter mixture and mix gently. Chill in the refrigerator for 1 hour. Shape into balls and roll in confectioners' sugar.

Makes 36 truffles

WHITE CHOCOLATE AVOCADO TRUFFLES

75 milliliters heavy cream
25 milliliters sweetened
    condensed milk
1 teaspoon vanilla extract
300 grams white chocolate,
    chopped
45 grams puréed ripe avocados
Roasted chopped cashews

Combine the cream, condensed milk and vanilla in a saucepan and bring just to a boil. Pour over the white chocolate in a heatproof bowl and whisk until the chocolate melts and the mixture is smooth. Stir in the avocado purée. Chill until firm.

Shape the mixture into small balls with a melon scooper or pipe into small balls with a pastry bag fitted with a plain tip. Place on a plate and chill until firm. Roll in cashews to coat.

Makes 25 truffles

IBM keypunch machines in use at Southern Pacific Railroad, 1915.

cookies

Family Picnic held in 1948 at the IBM Country Club in Poughkeepsie, New York.

FAMILY DAYS

For over sixty years, IBMers have been enjoying Family Day events.

These fun-filled days include everything from balloon-blowing contests

to vaudeville shows. The amusement park rides, cotton candy, ice

cream cones, barbecues, and picnics offer great opportunities for

IBMers to socialize with their co-workers and their families.

This tradition continues in many of our

IBM locations today.

Caramel Brownies 86

Chocolate Brownies 86

Chocolate Crunch Brownies 87

Kahlua Fudge Brownies 87

Mom's 1950 Chocolate
Brownies 88

White Chocolate Brownies 88

Creme de Menthe Squares 89

Fudge Bars 90

Peanut Butter Squares 91

Chocolate Chip Shortbread 91

Chocolate Walnut Squares 92

Ghirardelli Classic White Chip
Macadamia Bars 92

Chocolate Macaroon Squares 93

Magic Bars 93

Hazelnut Biscotti 94

Biscotti Alla Pennacchi 94

Black Forest Cookies 95

Chocolate Brownie Cookies 96

Buckaroons 96

Easy Chocolate Butter
Cookies 97

Chocolate Chip Cookies 97

Chocolate-Dipped Coconut
Macaroons 98

Chocolate Krispies 98

Kiss Cookies 100

Cracker Brittle 101

Brownie Balls 101

Chocolate Krinkles 102

Chocolate Chunk Macadamia
Cookies 103

First-Prize Chocolate
Mint Cookies 103

Chocolate Mint
Sugar Cookies 104

One-Minute Cookies 105

Mocha Slice Cookies 105

Easy Chocolate Nut Drops
with Creamy Fudge
Frosting 106

Chewy Milk Chocolate
Oatmeal Cookies 107

Chocolate and Oatmeal Peanut
Butter Cookies 107

Old-Fashioned Chocolate
Cookie Snaps 109

Pizzelle 109

CARAMEL BROWNIES

1/2 cup (1 stick) margarine
2/3 cup evaporated milk
1 (2-layer) package German
    chocolate cake mix
1 (14-ounce) package caramel
    candies
1 cup (6 ounces) chocolate chips
1/2 cup nuts (optional)

Microwave the margarine in a large microwave-safe bowl on High until melted. Stir in half the evaporated milk. Add the cake mix and mix well. Spread three-fourths of the batter in an ungreased 9×13-inch baking pan. Bake in a preheated 350-degree oven for 12 to 15 minutes.

Combine the caramels with the remaining evaporated milk in a microwave-safe bowl. Microwave on High for 2 minutes, stirring after each minute. Continue to microwave until the caramels melt completely, stirring every 30 seconds. Spread the mixture over the partially baked layer.

Sprinkle with the chocolate chips and nuts. Spoon the remaining cake batter over the top and press to cover evenly. Bake for 15 minutes longer. Cool in the pan on a wire rack. Cut into squares. Reduce the oven temperature to 340 degrees to bake in a glass baking dish.

Makes 2 1/2 dozen brownies

CHOCOLATE BROWNIES

1/2 cup (1 stick) butter
2 ounces unsweetened chocolate
1 cup sugar
2 eggs
1/2 teaspoon vanilla extract
1/4 cup all-purpose flour
1/4 teaspoon salt
1 cup chopped walnuts
1 cup (6 ounces) semisweet
    chocolate chips

Combine the butter and unsweetened chocolate in a saucepan. Heat over low heat until melted, stirring to blend well. Remove from the heat and add the sugar, eggs and vanilla; beat until smooth. Stir in the flour, salt, walnuts and chocolate chips.

Spoon into a buttered and floured 8×8-inch baking pan. Bake in a preheated 325-degree oven for 40 minutes. Cool in the pan on a wire rack and cut into squares.

Makes 16 brownies

CHOCOLATE CRUNCH BROWNIES

Cream the butter and sugar in a large mixing bowl until light and fluffy. Beat in the eggs. Stir in the flour, baking cocoa and vanilla.

Spoon into a greased 9×13-inch baking pan. Bake in a preheated 350-degree oven for 25 minutes. Cool in the pan on a wire rack. Spread with the marshmallow creme.

Combine the chocolate chips and peanut butter in a large saucepan. Heat over low heat until the chocolate chips melt, stirring to blend well. Remove from the heat and stir in the cereal. Spread over the marshmallow layer. Chill, covered, in the refrigerator until firm. Cut into squares and store in the refrigerator.

Makes 2 dozen brownies

1 cup (2 sticks) butter, softened
2 cups sugar
4 eggs
1 cup all-purpose flour
6 tablespoons baking cocoa
2 teaspoons vanilla extract
1 (7-ounce) jar marshmallow creme
2 cups (12 ounces) chocolate chips
1 cup creamy peanut butter
3 cups crisp rice cereal

KAHLUA FUDGE BROWNIES

Combine the butter and chocolate in a microwave-safe bowl. Microwave on High until the butter and chocolate melt, stirring to mix well. Beat the eggs with the sugar in a mixing bowl. Add the chocolate mixture, Kahlúa, flour, baking powder, salt and chopped pecans; mix well.

Spread in a greased 9×13-inch baking pan. Bake in a preheated 350-degree oven for 30 minutes. Top with the pecan halves and cool in the pan on a wire rack. Cut into squares.

Makes 2 dozen brownies

2/3 cup butter
3 ounces unsweetened chocolate
3 eggs
2 cups sugar
1/4 cup Kahlúa
1 1/2 cups all-purpose flour
1/2 teaspoon baking powder
1/2 teaspoon salt
3/4 cup chopped pecans
24 pecan halves

MOM'S 1950 CHOCOLATE BROWNIES

Brownies
1 3/4 cups all-purpose flour
1 teaspoon salt
1 cup (2 sticks) butter
4 ounces baking chocolate
2 1/4 cups sugar
2 teaspoons vanilla extract
5 eggs
1 cup chopped nuts

Cooked Fudge Frosting
2 cups sugar
1/4 teaspoon salt
2 ounces baking chocolate
1/4 cup light corn syrup
1/2 cup milk
1 teaspoon vanilla extract

Brownies
Sift the flour and salt together. Melt the butter with the chocolate in a saucepan over low heat, stirring to mix well. Beat in the sugar and vanilla. Beat the eggs in a mixing bowl. Add the chocolate mixture and mix well. Stir in the flour mixture and nuts.

Spoon into a buttered 12×18-inch baking pan. Bake in a preheated 350-degree oven for 25 minutes; do not overbake. Cool in the pan on a wire rack.

Frosting
Combine the sugar, salt, chocolate, corn syrup, milk and vanilla in a saucepan. Bring to a boil and boil for 1 to 2 minutes, stirring to mix well. Pour the hot frosting over the brownies. Cool to room temperature and cut into squares.

Serves 20

WHITE CHOCOLATE BROWNIES

6 ounces white chocolate
1 cup (2 sticks) unsalted butter
6 eggs
2 1/2 cups sugar
2 teaspoons vanilla extract
1 3/4 cups all-purpose flour, sifted
1/2 teaspoon salt
2 cups (12 ounces) white
    chocolate chips
2 cups walnuts, chopped (optional)

Melt the white chocolate and butter in a small saucepan over very low heat or in a double boiler over simmering water, stirring to mix well. Let cool slightly. Beat the eggs and sugar in a mixing bowl until thick and pale yellow. Mix in the vanilla. Stir in the chocolate mixture. Add the flour and salt and mix just until moistened; do not overmix. Stir in the white chocolate chips and walnuts.

Spoon into a buttered and lightly floured 10×15-inch baking pan, spreading evenly. Bake in a preheated 325-degree oven for 25 to 30 minutes or just until the center is set. Cool in the pan on a wire rack and cut into squares.

Makes 35 brownies

CRÈME DE MENTHE SQUARES

Crust
Combine the butter and baking cocoa in a saucepan. Heat until the butter melts, stirring to mix well. Remove from the heat and add the confectioners' sugar, egg and vanilla; mix well. Stir in the graham cracker crumbs. Press over the bottom of a 9×13-inch glass baking dish.

Crème de Menthe Filling
Combine 1/2 cup melted butter with the crème de menthe in a small mixing bowl. Beat in the confectioners' sugar at low speed. Spread over the graham cracker layer. Chill in the refrigerator for 1 hour.

Topping
Melt 1/4 cup butter with the chocolate chips in a small saucepan, stirring to mix well. Spread over the chilled layer. Chill for 1 to 2 hours. Let stand at room temperature for 1 hour or longer before cutting into small squares.

Makes 4 dozen squares

Chocolate Graham Cracker Crust
1/2 cup (1 stick) butter
1/2 cup baking cocoa
1/2 cup confectioners' sugar
1 egg, beaten
1 teaspoon vanilla extract
2 cups graham cracker crumbs

Crème de Menthe Filling
1/2 cup (1 stick) butter, melted
1/3 cup crème de menthe
3 cups confectioners' sugar

Topping
1/4 cup (1/2 stick) butter
1 1/2 cups (9 ounces) semisweet
   chocolate chips

*San Jose Family Day,
Wheelbarrow Races, 1956.*

FUDGE BARS

4 ounces bittersweet chocolate
1 cup (2 sticks) butter
4 eggs
2 cups sugar
1 cup all-purpose flour
Pinch of salt
2 teaspoons vanilla extract
2 cups chopped nuts (optional)

Melt the chocolate with the butter in a small saucepan over low heat or microwave until melted; stir to blend well. Beat the eggs with the sugar in a mixing bowl just until smooth; do not overbeat. Add the chocolate mixture and mix well. Add the flour, salt and vanilla; mix at low speed until smooth. Stir in the nuts.

Spoon into a 9×13-inch baking pan that has been buttered or sprayed with nonstick cooking spray. Bake in a preheated 325-degree oven for 25 to 30 minutes or just until firm; do not overbake. Cool in the pan on a wire rack. Cut into bars.

Makes 2 dozen bars

Lori Bolton enjoying herself at an IBM Canada employee year-end holiday party in 1959.

PEANUT BUTTER SQUARES

Combine the graham cracker crumbs, butter, confectioners' sugar and peanut butter in a bowl and mix well. Press into a buttered 9×13-inch pan.

Microwave the chocolate chips in a microwave-safe bowl until melted; stir until smooth. Spread over the graham cracker layer. Let stand until the chocolate is cool. Cut into squares in the pan. Freeze until the chocolate is firm. Store in the freezer.

These are even good served frozen, especially in the summer.

Makes 2 dozen squares

1^1/2 cups (5 to 6 ounces) graham cracker crumbs
^{2}/3 cup butter, melted
3 cups confectioners' sugar, sifted
1^1/2 cups peanut butter
2 cups (12 ounces) semisweet chocolate chips, or to taste

CHOCOLATE CHIP SHORTBREAD

Cream the butter and sugar in a large mixing bowl until light and fluffy. Add the flour and cornstarch and mix well. Stir in the chocolate chips.

Press the mixture into an ungreased 9×13-inch baking pan. Pierce all over with a fork. Bake in a preheated 350-degree oven for 35 to 45 minutes or just until the edges begin to brown; cover with foil if the shortbread appears to be browning too rapidly. Cool in the pan for 15 minutes. Cut into bars while still warm.

Do not substitute any other form of shortening for the unsalted butter in this recipe.

Makes 3 dozen bars

1 cup (2 sticks) unsalted butter, softened
^{1}/3 cup sugar
1^3/4 cups all-purpose flour
^{1}/4 cup cornstarch
1 cup (6 ounces) miniature chocolate chips

CHOCOLATE WALNUT SQUARES

1/2 cup (1 stick) butter, softened
1/4 cup sugar
11/4 cups all-purpose flour
1/4 cup (1/2 stick) butter
1/2 cup sugar
2 tablespoons heavy cream
13/4 cups coarsely chopped walnuts
1 cup flaked coconut
4 ounces semisweet chocolate,
   coarsely chopped

Cream 1/2 cup butter and 1/4 cup sugar in a mixing bowl until light and fluffy. Add the flour and mix well. Press into an ungreased 9×9-inch baking pan. Bake in a preheated 350-degree oven for 15 minutes or just until the edges are light brown.

Combine 1/4 cup butter and 1/2 cup sugar with the cream in a saucepan. Heat until the butter melts and the sugar dissolves, stirring to mix well. Stir in the walnuts.

Sprinkle the coconut and chocolate over the baked layer and spread the walnut mixture over the top. Bake for 20 minutes longer or until golden brown. Cool in the pan on a wire rack and cut into squares.

Makes 1 dozen squares

GHIRARDELLI CLASSIC WHITE CHIP MACADAMIA BARS

1 cup (2 sticks) butter, softened
11/2 cups packed light brown sugar
2 teaspoons vanilla extract
2 eggs
21/4 cups all-purpose flour
11/2 teaspoons baking powder
1 teaspoon salt
2 cups (12 ounces) Ghirardelli white
   chocolate chips
1 cup macadamia nuts,
   coarsely chopped

Combine the butter and brown sugar in a large mixing bowl and beat at medium speed for 4 minutes or until light and fluffy. Mix in the vanilla. Add the eggs one at a time, mixing at low speed until smooth. Add the flour, baking powder and salt gradually, mixing well at low speed. Fold in the white chocolate chips and macadamia nuts.

Spread in a 9×13-inch pan that has been buttered or sprayed with nonstick cooking spray. Bake in a preheated 325-degree oven for 25 to 30 minutes or until golden brown. Cool in the pan on a wire rack and cut into bars.

Makes 2 dozen bars

CHOCOLATE MACAROON SQUARES

Combine the crushed graham crackers with the butter and 2 eggs in a mixing bowl; mix well. Press into an ungreased 9×13-inch baking pan. Combine the condensed milk, 2 eggs and the vanilla in a bowl and mix well. Stir in 1 cup coconut, the chocolate chips and pecans. Spread evenly over the graham cracker layer. Sprinkle with 1 cup coconut.

Bake in a preheated 350-degree oven for 40 to 45 minutes or just until the coconut begins to brown. Cool in the pan on a wire rack. Cut into squares.

Makes 20 squares

18 graham crackers, very
   finely crushed
1/4 cup (1/2 stick) butter, softened
2 eggs
2 (14-ounce) cans sweetened
   condensed milk
2 eggs
2 teaspoons vanilla extract
1 cup flaked sweetened coconut
2 cups (12 ounces) semisweet
   chocolate chips
1 cup chopped pecans
1 cup flaked sweetened coconut

MAGIC BARS

Spread the melted butter in a 9×13-inch baking pan. Sprinkle the graham cracker crumbs evenly over the butter. Layer the walnuts, chocolate chips and coconut over the graham cracker crumbs.

Pour the condensed milk evenly over the layers. Bake in a preheated 350-degree oven for 20 minutes. Cool in the pan on a wire rack and cut into bars.

Makes 2 dozen bars

1/2 cup (1 stick) butter, melted
1 1/2 cups graham cracker crumbs
1 cup chopped walnuts
1 cup (6 ounces) chocolate chips
1 1/3 cups (3 1/2 ounces)
   flaked coconut
1 1/2 cups sweetened
   condensed milk

HAZELNUT BISCOTTI

4 cups all-purpose flour
2 teaspoons baking powder
1/4 teaspoon salt
4 eggs
1 cup sugar
1 cup vegetable oil
2 teaspoons vanilla extract
3/4 cup chopped roasted hazelnuts
3/4 cup (4 1/2 ounces) semisweet
    chocolate chips

Mix the flour, baking powder and salt together. Combine the eggs, sugar and oil in a mixing bowl and beat for 5 minutes. Add the dry ingredients and vanilla and mix well. Stir in the hazelnuts and chocolate chips.

Shape into two loaves with oiled hands and place on a cookie sheet. Bake in a preheated 350-degree oven for 30 minutes. Cool on a wire rack. Slice the loaves diagonally. Place the slices cut side down on the cookie sheet. Bake for 20 minutes longer or until light brown.

Makes 40 biscotti

BISCOTTI ALLA PENNACCHI

4 cups all-purpose flour
4 teaspoons baking powder
1/4 cup Dutch-process baking
    cocoa (optional)
4 eggs
1 1/3 cups sugar
1/2 cup canola oil
1 tablespoon vanilla extract
1 tablespoon anise or
    almond flavoring
3/4 cup sliced almonds, or 1 cup
    chopped walnuts or pistachios
1 tablespoon anise seeds
1/2 cup (3 ounces) milk chocolate
    chips, semisweet chocolate
    chips or white chocolate chips

Sift the flour, baking powder and baking cocoa together. Beat the eggs with the sugar in a mixing bowl until thick and pale yellow. Beat in the canola oil and flavorings. Add the dry ingredients and mix well. Fold in the almonds and anise seeds.

Divide the dough into eight portions. Flatten and shape each portion into a rectangle 1/4 to 1/2 inch thick on a floured surface. Place on a greased cookie sheet. Bake in a preheated 375-degree oven for 20 minutes or until golden brown. Cool on the cookie sheet on a wire rack.

Reduce the oven temperature to 300 degrees. Cut each rectangle diagonally into slices 1/2 to 3/4 inch wide with a serrated knife. Place the slices cut side down on an ungreased cookie sheet. Toast for 5 to 10 minutes or until light brown.

Melt the chocolate chips in a double boiler over simmering water. Dip half of each toasted slice into the chocolate and place on a wire rack or baking parchment; let stand until the chocolate is firm. Store in an airtight container.

Makes 3 dozen biscotti

BLACK FOREST COOKIES

Whisk the flour, baking cocoa, baking powder and salt together in a medium bowl. Combine the chopped chocolate with the butter in a large heatproof bowl and place over a saucepan of simmering water. Heat until the chocolate and butter melt, stirring to blend well.

Remove from the heat and whisk in the granulated sugar, brown sugar and eggs. Add the dry ingredients and whisk just until combined; do not overmix. Fold in the chocolate chunks and dried cherries. Place plastic wrap directly on the surface of the mixture and chill for 30 to 45 minutes or until firm.

Drop into mounds equal to 2 level tablespoons 2 inches apart onto baking parchment-lined cookie sheets. Bake in a preheated 350-degree oven for 11 to 13 minutes or just until the edges are set but not brown. Cool on the cookie sheets for 1 to 2 minutes and remove to a wire rack to cool completely.

Makes 3 dozen cookies

1 cup all-purpose flour
2 tablespoons baking cocoa
1 teaspoon baking powder
1/2 teaspoon salt (optional)
8 ounces semisweet chocolate or bittersweet chocolate, chopped
1/2 cup (1 stick) butter, chopped
1/2 cup granulated sugar
1/4 cup packed dark brown sugar
2 eggs
2 cups (12 ounces) semisweet chocolate chunks
11/2 cups dried cherries or cherry-flavor dried cranberries

IBM Family Dinner in Taiwan, 1962.

CHOCOLATE BROWNIE COOKIES

1/4 cup all-purpose flour
1/4 teaspoon baking powder
1/8 teaspoon salt
5 ounces bittersweet
    chocolate, chopped
2 ounces unsweetened baking
    chocolate, chopped
2 tablespoons butter
1/2 teaspoon instant
    espresso granules
1 1/2 teaspoons water
2 eggs, at room temperature
2/3 cup granulated sugar
1 teaspoon vanilla extract
1/4 cup (1 1/2 ounces) miniature
    chocolate chips
Confectioners' sugar, for garnish

Mix the flour, baking powder and salt together. Combine the bittersweet chocolate, unsweetened chocolate and butter in a microwave-safe bowl. Microwave on Medium for 1 1/2 to 2 minutes or until melted; stir to blend well.

Dissolve the espresso granules in the water in a large mixing bowl. Add the eggs, granulated sugar and vanilla and beat for 5 minutes or until thickened and tripled in volume. Fold in the chocolate mixture gently with a spatula; some streaks may remain. Fold in the dry ingredients and then the chocolate chips. Let stand for 15 to 20 minutes or until slightly thickened.

Drop by heaping teaspoonfuls 1 inch apart onto cookie sheets lined with baking parchment or foil. Bake in a preheated 375-degree oven for 8 to 9 minutes or until the tops of the cookies are puffed and cracked. Cool on the cookie sheets. Garnish with confectioners' sugar.

Makes 3 dozen cookies

BUCKAROONS

2 cups all-purpose flour
1/2 teaspoon baking powder
1 teaspoon baking soda
1/2 teaspoon salt
1 cup shortening
1 cup granulated sugar
1 cup packed brown sugar
2 eggs
2 cups rolled oats
2 cups (12 ounces) chocolate chips,
    or to taste
Chopped nuts (optional)
1 teaspoon vanilla extract
Milk (optional)

Sift the flour, baking powder, baking soda and salt together. Cream the shortening with the granulated sugar and brown sugar in a mixing bowl until light and fluffy. Beat in the eggs. Add the sifted ingredients and mix well. Stir in the oats, chocolate chips, nuts and vanilla. Add a small amount of milk if the mixture appears too crumbly.

Drop onto cookie sheets. Bake in a preheated 350-degree oven for 15 minutes or until golden brown. Cool on the cookie sheets for 5 minutes and remove to a wire rack to cool completely.

Makes 4 to 5 dozen cookies

EASY CHOCOLATE BUTTER COOKIES

Combine the cream cheese and butter in a mixing bowl and beat until light and fluffy. Beat in the egg and vanilla. Add the cake mix and mix to form a stiff dough; do not overmix. Chill in the refrigerator for 2 hours or longer.

Shape by tablespoonfuls into balls and roll in confectioners' sugar. Place 2 inches apart on ungreased cookie sheets. Bake in a preheated 350-degree oven for 10 to 12 minutes or until firm. Cool on the cookie sheets until cool enough to handle and remove to a wire rack to cool completely. Dust with additional confectioners' sugar.

Makes 2 dozen cookies

8 ounces cream cheese, softened
1/2 cup (1 stick) unsalted
    butter, softened
1 egg
1 teaspoon vanilla extract
1 (2-layer) package moist chocolate
    cake mix
Confectioners' sugar

CHOCOLATE CHIP COOKIES

Sift the flour and baking soda together. Cream the shortening, butter, granulated sugar and brown sugar in a mixing bowl until light and fluffy. Beat in the eggs and vanilla. Add the flour mixture and mix well. Stir in the chocolate chips.

Drop by teaspoonfuls or tablespoonfuls onto an ungreased cookie sheet. Bake in a preheated 375-degree oven for 10 minutes or until light brown. Cool on the cookie sheet for several minutes and remove to a wire rack to cool completely.

Makes 3 dozen cookies

3 cups all-purpose flour
1 teaspoon baking soda
1 cup shortening
1/3 cup butter, softened
1 cup granulated sugar
1 cup packed brown sugar
2 eggs
2 teaspoons vanilla extract
2 cups (12 ounces) chocolate chips

cookies 97

CHOCOLATE-DIPPED COCONUT MACAROONS

1 (14-ounce) package flaked
   coconut, about 5 1/3 cups
2/3 cup sugar
6 tablespoons all-purpose flour
1/4 teaspoon salt
4 egg whites
1 teaspoon almond extract
8 ounces semisweet
   chocolate, melted

Mix the coconut, sugar, flour and salt in a large bowl. Add the egg whites and almond extract and mix well. Drop by tablespoonfuls onto greased and floured cookie sheets. Bake in a preheated 325-degree oven for 20 minutes or until the edges are golden brown. Remove immediately to a wire rack to cool completely.

Dip the cookies into the melted chocolate and place on waxed paper. Let stand at room temperature until the chocolate is firm or chill in the refrigerator for 30 minutes.

Serves 4 to 6

CHOCOLATE KRISPIES

12 ounces dark chocolate
6 cups crisp rice cereal
4 cups miniature marshmallows

Melt the chocolate in a saucepan over low heat, stirring until smooth. Add the cereal and stir to coat evenly. Stir in the marshmallows. Spoon into paper-lined muffin cups and chill in the refrigerator.

Makes 1 dozen krispies

Thomas J. Watson, Sr., enjoys the company of the Blakely family and others at IBM Poughkeepsie's Family Day celebration held on September 4, 1956.

KISS COOKIES

1 cup shortening
1 cup peanut butter
1 cup granulated sugar
1 cup packed brown sugar
2 eggs
1 teaspoon vanilla extract
2 1/2 cups all-purpose flour
1/2 teaspoon baking powder
3/4 teaspoon baking soda
1/2 teaspoon salt
Granulated sugar
60 Hershey's kisses or miniature
    Reese's peanut butter cups

Cream the shortening with the peanut butter, 1 cup granulated sugar and the brown sugar until light and fluffy.

Beat in the eggs and vanilla. Add the flour, baking powder, baking soda and salt and mix well. Cover with plastic wrap and chill in the refrigerator for 15 minutes. Shape the mixture into balls and roll in additional granulated sugar.

Place the balls in miniature muffin cups or on cookie sheets. Bake in a preheated 375-degree oven for 10 minutes; the cookies will have small cracks. Remove from the oven and press a kiss into the center of each cookie. Let cool in the muffin cups or on the cookie sheet for 2 minutes; remove to a wire rack to cool completely. Store in an airtight container with a slice of bread to maintain moisture.

Makes 5 dozen cookies

CRACKER BRITTLE

Spray a large cookie sheet with nonstick cooking spray; line it with foil and spray the foil. Arrange the crackers on the prepared cookie sheet. Melt the butter with the sugar in a small saucepan over low heat and cook until frothy. Remove from the heat and stir in the vanilla. Return to the heat for several minutes, stirring constantly. Pour over the crackers. Bake in a preheated 325-degree oven for 8 to 10 minutes or until a light caramel color. Let cool on a wire rack.

Sprinkle with the chocolate chips and return to the oven for 1 to 2 minutes or just until the chocolate chips melt; spread the chocolate evenly with a spatula. Sprinkle with the nuts. Chill until the chocolate is set. Remove with the foil and break into pieces.

Serves 12 to 15

1 sleeve saltine crackers, or
    6 sheets matzo
1 cup (2 sticks) butter or 1 cup soft
    butter with canola oil
$1/2$ cup sugar
2 teaspoons vanilla extract
2 to $2^{2}/3$ cups (12 to 16 ounces)
    chocolate chips
1 to 2 cups chopped nuts (optional)

BROWNIE BALLS

Mix the flour, baking powder and salt together. Cream the shortening in a mixing bowl until light. Add 2 cups sugar and beat until fluffy. Beat in the eggs and chocolate. Add the flour mixture gradually, mixing at low speed until smooth.

Spread in a 9×13-inch baking pan sprayed with nonstick cooking spray. Bake in a preheated 350-degree oven for 30 minutes or just until set; if the edges are brown and pulling from the sides of the pan, the mixture has been baked too long. Let cool in the pan just until warm.

Scoop out walnut-size portions and shape into balls with the hands. Roll the balls in $1/2$ to $3/4$ cup sugar in a bowl, coating evenly. Let cool completely on a wire rack. Store in an airtight container for no more than several days.

Makes 30 to 40 cookies

$1^{1}/2$ cups all-purpose flour
$1/2$ teaspoon baking powder
$1/2$ teaspoon salt
1 cup shortening
2 cups sugar
4 eggs, beaten
4 ounces unsweetened baking
    chocolate, melted
$1/2$ to $3/4$ cup sugar

CHOCOLATE KRINKLES

2 cups all-purpose flour
6 tablespoons baking cocoa
2 teaspoons baking powder
1/2 teaspoon salt
1/2 cup shortening
1³/4 cups confectioners' sugar
²/3 cup granulated sugar
2 eggs, beaten
2 teaspoons vanilla extract
1/3 cup milk
1/2 cup chopped pecans, walnuts
    or macadamia nuts
1 cup confectioners' sugar

Sift the flour, baking cocoa, baking powder and salt together. Cream the shortening with 1³/4 cups confectioners' sugar and the granulated sugar in a mixing bowl until light and fluffy. Beat in the eggs and vanilla. Add the sifted ingredients alternately with the milk, mixing well after each addition. Stir in the pecans. Cover loosely and chill in the refrigerator for 3 hours or longer.

Shape the dough into balls the size of small walnuts. Roll in 1 cup confectioners' sugar. Place on an ungreased cookie sheet. Bake in a preheated 350-degree oven for 10 to 15 minutes or until the cookies flatten and crinkle. Remove to a wire rack to cool.

Makes 5 dozen cookies

Marilyn Smith, Barbara Brook, and Nancy Bradt savor cotton candy between rides at IBM Endicott's Family Day celebration in 1955.

CHOCOLATE CHUNK MACADAMIA COOKIES

Combine the butter, granulated sugar, brown sugar, egg and vanilla in a large mixing bowl. Beat at medium-high speed until smooth. Reduce the mixer speed to low and add the flour. Increase the speed gradually and beat just until blended. Stir in the chocolate, coconut and macadamia nuts.

Drop by heaping tablespoonfuls 2^1/$_2$ inches apart onto greased cookie sheets. Bake one sheet at a time in a preheated 325-degree oven for 17 minutes or just until the edges are light brown and the tops appear dry. Let cool on the cookie sheet for 5 minutes and remove to a wire rack to cool completely.

Makes 22 cookies

^{2}/$_3$ cup butter or margarine,
    softened
^{2}/$_3$ cup granulated sugar
^{1}/$_2$ cup packed dark brown sugar
1 egg
1 teaspoon vanilla extract
1^1/$_2$ cups all-purpose flour
9 ounces dark chocolate, chopped
    into ^{1}/$_2$-inch pieces
1^1/$_2$ cups flaked coconut
^{3}/$_4$ cup chopped macadamia nuts

FIRST-PRIZE CHOCOLATE MINT COOKIES

Mix the flour, baking soda and salt together. Combine the margarine, brown sugar and water in a large saucepan and heat over low heat until the margarine melts, stirring to blend well. Remove from the heat and add the chocolate chips. Stir until the chocolate chips melt. Pour into a large mixing bowl and let cool for 10 minutes. Beat in the eggs one at a time at high speed. Reduce the mixer speed to low and add the flour mixture, beating until smooth. Chill in the refrigerator for 2 hours or longer.

Shape the dough by tablespoonfuls into balls and place 2 inches apart on foil-lined cookie sheets. Bake in a preheated 350-degree oven for no longer than 12 minutes; the cookies will become crisp as they cool. Place one chocolate mint on each hot cookie immediately. Let stand for 1 minute to melt the candy and spread with a knife to cover each cookie. Chill in the refrigerator until the mint topping is firm.

Makes 5 to 6 dozen cookies

2^1/$_2$ cups all-purpose flour
1^1/$_4$ teaspoons baking soda
^{1}/$_2$ teaspoon salt
^{3}/$_4$ cup (1^1/$_2$ sticks) margarine
1^1/$_2$ cups packed light brown sugar
2^1/$_2$ tablespoons water
2 cups (12 ounces) semisweet
    chocolate chips
2 eggs
5 to 6 dozen Andes crème
    de menthe candy wafers

CHOCOLATE MINT SUGAR COOKIES

2 1/2 cups all-purpose flour
1 1/2 teaspoons baking powder
3/4 teaspoon salt
3/4 cup vegetable oil
1 cup sugar
2 eggs
1 teaspoon vanilla extract
1 2/3 cups (10 ounces) mint
    chocolate chips
1/4 cup sugar

Mix the flour, baking powder and salt together. Combine the oil and 1 cup sugar in a large bowl and mix well. Beat in the eggs and vanilla. Add the flour mixture and mix well. Stir in the mint chocolate chips.

Shape into small balls and roll in 1/4 cup sugar. Place on an ungreased cookie sheet and bake in a preheated 350-degree oven for 8 to 10 minutes or until golden brown. Remove to a wire rack to cool.

Makes 4 dozen cookies

Attendees at the IBM Rochester, Minnesota, facility's Open House in 1958.

ONE-MINUTE COOKIES

Combine the sugar, baking cocoa, milk and margarine in a saucepan. Bring to a boil and boil for 1 minute. Stir in the oats, peanut butter, coconut and vanilla. Drop by teaspoonfuls onto waxed paper. Let stand until cool.

Makes 1 dozen cookies

1 cup sugar
1/4 cup baking cocoa
1/4 cup milk
1/4 cup (1/2 stick) margarine
1 cup quick-cooking oats
1/4 cup peanut butter
1/4 cup flaked coconut
1/2 teaspoon vanilla extract

MOCHA SLICE COOKIES

Sift the flour, baking cocoa, espresso granules, cinnamon and salt together. Cream the butter and granulated sugar with a paddle attachment in a mixing bowl until light and fluffy. Beat in the egg and vanilla. Add the flour mixture gradually, mixing at low speed. Stir in the cocoa nibs.

Shape into a log 2 inches in diameter on a lightly floured surface. Wrap in baking parchment and chill in the refrigerator for 1 hour or until firm. Unwrap the log and let stand at room temperature for 5 minutes. Brush with water and roll in sanding sugar, coating evenly. Cut into 1/4-inch slices.

Arrange the slices cut side down 2 inches apart on a baking parchment-lined cookie sheet. Bake in a preheated 350-degree oven for 10 minutes or until the centers of the cookies are set. Remove to a wire rack to cool completely.

Cocoa nibs are roasted cocoa beans that have been separated from their husks and broken into small bits. Sanding sugar is a coarse sugar that comes in various colors for decorating.

Makes 4 dozen cookies

11/2 cups all-purpose flour
3/4 cup baking cocoa
2 tablespoons instant espresso granules or coffee granules
Ground cinnamon to taste
1/4 teaspoon salt
3/4 cup (11/2 sticks) unsalted butter, softened
1 cup granulated sugar
1 egg
1 teaspoon vanilla extract
1/2 cup cocoa nibs
Sanding sugar

EASY CHOCOLATE NUT DROPS WITH CREAMY FUDGE FROSTING

Cookies

1 3/4 cups all-purpose flour
1/2 teaspoon baking soda
1/2 teaspoon salt
2/3 cup shortening
1 cup packed brown sugar
1 egg
1/2 cup milk
1 teaspoon vanilla extract
2 ounces unsweetened baking
    chocolate, melted
1/2 cup chopped walnuts (optional)

Creamy Fudge Frosting

3 ounces unsweetened
    baking chocolate
1/4 cup (1/2 stick) butter
2 cups (or more) confectioners'
    sugar, sifted
1/8 teaspoon salt
1 teaspoon vanilla extract
1/3 cup milk or cream, heated
Walnut halves (optional)

Cookies

Sift the flour, baking soda and salt into a large bowl. Add the shortening, brown sugar, egg, milk and vanilla. Beat at medium speed for 1 to 2 minutes or until smooth. Add the melted chocolate and walnuts; beat for 1 minute or until well mixed.

Drop by rounded teaspoonfuls onto a greased cookie sheet. Bake in a preheated 350-degree oven for 15 minutes. Remove to a wire rack to cool.

Frosting

Melt the chocolate with the butter in a double boiler over simmering water, stirring to blend well. Combine the confectioners' sugar with the salt, vanilla and hot milk in a large mixing bowl; beat until smooth. Beat in the chocolate mixture, adding additional confectioners' sugar if necessary for the desired consistency. Spread thickly on each cookie and top each with a walnut half.

Makes 4 to 6 dozen cookies

Thomas J. Watson, Sr., with employee James E. Burgess, Sr., and family at IBM Family Day Picnic, Poughkeepsie, New York, 1946.

CHEWY MILK CHOCOLATE OATMEAL COOKIES

Mix the oats, flour, baking soda and salt together. Cream the butter, granulated sugar and brown sugar in a bowl until light and fluffy. Beat in the egg and vanilla. Add the oats mixture and mix well. Stir in the baking bits.

Drop by rounded tablespoonfuls 2 inches apart onto an ungreased cookie sheet. Bake in a preheated 375-degree oven for 8 to 9 minutes or just until set; do not overbake. Let cool on the cookie sheet for 1 minute and remove to a wire rack to cool completely.

Makes 4 dozen cookies

3 cups quick-cooking oats or rolled oats
1 1/2 cups all-purpose flour
1 teaspoon baking soda
1 teaspoon salt
1 1/4 cups (2 1/2 sticks) butter or margarine, softened
1/2 cup granulated sugar
3/4 cup packed light brown sugar
1 egg
1 1/2 teaspoons vanilla extract
1 3/4 cups "M & M's" miniature milk chocolate baking bits

CHOCOLATE AND OATMEAL PEANUT BUTTER COOKIES

Combine the sugar, baking cocoa, butter and milk in a saucepan. Bring to a boil and boil for 1 1/2 minutes, stirring to blend well. Remove from the heat and add the oats; mix well. Stir in the peanut butter and vanilla. Drop by spoonfuls onto waxed paper. Let stand for 5 to 10 minutes or until firm.

You can also add coconut and/or raisins to this recipe, if desired.

Makes 2 dozen cookies

2 cups sugar
1 tablespoon baking cocoa
1/2 cup (1 stick) butter or margarine
1/2 cup milk
2 1/2 cups quick-cooking oats
1/2 cup creamy or chunky peanut butter
1 teaspoon vanilla extract

Thomas Watson, Sr., greets the Jamison family at the IBM Poughkeepsie, New York, Family Picnic on September 7, 1946.

Old-Fashioned Chocolate Cookie Snaps

Mix the flour, baking soda and salt in a small bowl. Cream the shortening, 1 cup sugar and the egg at low speed in a mixing bowl until light and fluffy. Add the corn syrup and chocolate and mix well. Stir in the dry ingredients by hand.

Shape into 1-inch balls. Roll in 1/2 cup sugar and place 2 inches apart on an ungreased cookie sheet. Bake in a preheated 350-degree oven for 15 minutes. Let cool on the cookie sheet for several minutes and remove to a wire rack to cool completely.

You can prepare the cookie dough and store it in the refrigerator for up to 5 days.

Makes 1 1/2 dozen cookies

1 3/4 cups all-purpose flour
2 teaspoons baking soda
1/4 teaspoon salt
3/4 cup shortening, or 1 1/2 sticks margarine, softened
1 cup sugar
1 egg
1/4 cup corn syrup
2 ounces chocolate, melted
1/2 cup sugar

Pizzelle

Sift the flour, baking powder and baking cocoa together. Beat the eggs in a mixing bowl, adding the sugar gradually. Add the canola oil and beat until smooth. Add the butter and flavorings. Add the dry ingredients and mix well. Stir in the anise seeds; the dough will be sticky.

Drop 1 tablespoon of the dough from a greased tablespoon or scoop into the center of each grid in a pizzelle iron. Bake for 30 seconds on the timer or until golden brown. Let cool completely.

Melt the chocolate chips in a double boiler over simmering water, stirring until smooth. Dip half of each pizzelle into the melted chocolate. Place on a wire rack or baking parchment and let stand until the chocolate is firm. Store in an airtight container.

Makes 3 dozen

4 cups all-purpose flour
2 teaspoons baking powder
1/4 cup Dutch-process baking cocoa (optional)
6 large eggs, or 7 small eggs
1 1/2 cups sugar
1/2 cup canola oil
1/2 cup (1 stick) butter, melted and cooled
1 tablespoon vanilla extract
1 tablespoon lemon extract
10 drops of anise oil, or 1 tablespoon anise extract
1 tablespoon anise seeds
1/2 cup (3 ounces) milk chocolate chips, semisweet chocolate chips or white chocolate chips

pies & pastries

It's sometime in 1924, and four proud IBM salesmen stand outside the company's branch office in the Equitable Building at 816 Fourteenth Street, N.W., in Washington, D.C. This was the year in which the company's name was changed from the Computing-Tabulating-Recording Company to International Business Machines, and the branch's signage includes both names, as well as several of the company's components, such as the International Time Recording Company.

GLOBAL REACH

Naming a company International Business Machines when it is still

a relatively small upstart shows a definite vision for where that

company should go. And where IBM has gone is practically

everywhere. Today we operate in 170 countries, and about 60 percent

of our revenue comes from outside the United States. Even from the

early days, IBM has led the way to break down borders and include the

whole world in our strategy. Obviously, we

are more than international; we are global.

Chocolate Almond Pie 114

Chocolate Pie 114

Chocolate Chess Pie 116

Southern Chocolate
Chess Pie 117

Grandmother's
Chocolate Pie 118

Hot Fudge Pie 118

Fudge Walnut Brownie Pie 120

Chocolate Marvel Pie 121

Chocolate Mousse Pie 122

Chocolate Peanut Butter Pie 124

Creamy Chocolate
Mousse Pie 125

Triple-Layer Mud Pie 125

Chocolate Peanut Butter
Cookie Pie 127

Chocolate Pecan Pie 127

Chocolate Silk Pie 128

Choco-Baklava 129

Chocolate Coconut Phyllo
Triangles 130

Fondant Pastry 131

Fudge Brownie Cups 132

White Chocolate
Mousse Pastries 133

CHOCOLATE ALMOND PIE

1 giant Hershey's chocolate almond
    bar or Hershey's Symphony bar
12 ounces whipped topping
1 graham cracker pie shell with
    plastic cover

Break the chocolate bar into pieces and place in a medium saucepan. Melt over low heat, stirring until smooth. Remove from the heat and mix immediately with the whipped topping in a bowl.

Pour the chocolate filling into the pie shell and replace the plastic cover from the pie shell. Chill for 1 hour or longer before serving.

Serves 8

CHOCOLATE PIE

1 cup (6 ounces) chocolate chips
3 tablespoons butter
4 cups (1 quart) milk
1/2 cup cornstarch
1/2 cup sugar
3 extra-large eggs
1 teaspoon vanilla extract
1 baked (9-inch) pie shell

Melt the chocolate chips with the butter in a double boiler, stirring to blend well. Add 3 cups of the milk and bring to a boil. Blend the remaining 1 cup milk with the cornstarch in a bowl. Add to the boiling mixture and cook until thickened, stirring constantly. Add the sugar and cook until the sugar dissolves, stirring constantly. Remove from the heat.

Beat the eggs with the vanilla in a mixing bowl. Add half the chocolate mixture gradually, stirring to mix well. Stir into the remaining chocolate mixture in the double boiler. Cook over simmering water for 5 minutes, stirring constantly. Spoon into the pie shell and chill in the refrigerator. Serve with whipped cream if desired.

Serves 8

Seen here in 1948 is IBM's World Headquarters at 590 Madison Avenue in New York City.
The twenty-story, 100,000-square-foot building was dedicated in January 1938. It housed all
executive functions, as well as the sales and services departments serving the New York area.
This building was demolished beginning in 1977 to pave the way for construction on the same site,
starting in 1978, of a forty-three-story, five-sided IBM regional headquarters.

CHOCOLATE CHESS PIE

3/4 cup (1 1/2 sticks) butter
3 ounces unsweetened
    baking chocolate
1 cup sugar
3 eggs
1 tablespoon vanilla extract
Pinch of salt
1 unbaked (9-inch) pie shell

Melt the butter and chocolate in a double boiler over simmering water. Add the sugar, eggs, vanilla and salt and mix well.

Spoon the mixture into the pie shell. Bake in a preheated 350-degree oven for 30 to 40 minutes or until a wooden pick inserted near the center comes out clean. Chill in the refrigerator for 8 hours or longer. Serve cold.

Serves 8

The Computing-Tabulating-Recording Company is renamed International Business Machines Corporation (IBM) in 1924. The company had operated under the IBM name in Canada since 1917.

Southern Chocolate Chess Pie

Combine the butter, eggs, sugar, baking cocoa, cornmeal, salt, cream, lemon juice and vanilla in a large mixing bowl and mix well.

Spoon the mixture into the pie shell. Bake in a preheated 350-degree (180-degree C) oven for 30 to 35 minutes or until the crust is golden brown and a knife inserted near the center comes out clean. Cool on a wire rack. Serve with sweetened whipped cream if desired.

Serves 8

3/4 cup (11/2 sticks) butter, melted
4 eggs, beaten
11/2 cups sugar
3 tablespoons baking cocoa
2 teaspoons cornmeal
1/4 teaspoon salt
4 teaspoons whipping cream or
　　half-and-half
1/3 cup lemon juice (optional)
1 teaspoon vanilla extract
1 unbaked (9-inch) pie shell

Demonstration of the IBM 026 at the Taiwan Service Bureau, 1960.

GRANDMOTHER'S CHOCOLATE PIE

2 ounces unsweetened baking
    chocolate
1 (14-ounce) can sweetened
    condensed milk
1/4 cup cold water
1 teaspoon vanilla extract
1 baked (9-inch) pie shell
Whipped topping
Strawberries or blueberries,
    for garnish

Melt the chocolate in a double boiler over simmering water. Stir in the condensed milk. Cook until the mixture becomes dark and has the consistency of fudge before it is poured, stirring occasionally. Stir in the water. Cook until thickened, stirring occasionally. Remove from the heat and stir in the vanilla.

Spoon the mixture into the pie shell. Let stand at room temperature for 1 hour or longer. Top each serving with whipped topping and garnish with strawberries.

Serves 6 to 8

HOT FUDGE PIE

1/2 cup (1 stick) butter
3 ounces unsweetened
    baking chocolate
4 eggs
3 tablespoons light corn syrup
11/2 cups sugar
1/4 teaspoon salt
1 tablespoon vanilla extract
1 unbaked (9-inch) pie shell
Vanilla ice cream
Fresh raspberries, for garnish

Melt the butter in a double boiler over simmering water or in the microwave. Add the chocolate and stir until the chocolate melts and blends well. Let cool to room temperature.

Whisk the eggs in a bowl until smooth. Add the corn syrup, sugar, salt and vanilla and whisk to mix well. Whisk in the chocolate mixture.

Spoon the mixture into the pie shell. Bake in a preheated 350-degree oven for 45 minutes or until the top is puffed. Serve warm topped with vanilla ice cream. Garnish with raspberries.

Serves 8 to 10

Tribute Dinner at the Ambassador Hotel, Bombay, India, April 30, 1954.
From left to right: Mrs. P. R. V. Kukde; H. M. Frenchman; Miss J. M. Avon.

FUDGE WALNUT BROWNIE PIE

2/3 cup all-purpose flour

1/3 cup baking cocoa

1/4 teaspoon salt

2 eggs

1 cup sugar

1/2 cup (1 stick) butter, melted

1 teaspoon vanilla extract

1 cup (6 ounces) semisweet
    chocolate chips

1/2 cup chopped walnuts

Mix the flour, baking cocoa and salt together. Beat the eggs in a large bowl. Stir in the sugar, butter and vanilla. Add the dry ingredients and mix well. Stir in the chocolate chips and walnuts.

Spoon the mixture into a lightly greased 9-inch pie plate. Bake in a preheated 350-degree oven for 30 minutes or until set. Serve warm or let cool to room temperature. Serve with whipped cream or ice cream if desired.

Serves 6 to 8

Attendees at IBM 1950 Hundred Percent Club meeting in Windsor, Canada, March 30, 1951. Arthur K. Watson, President of IBM World Trade Corporation, is seated at the head table.

CHOCOLATE MARVEL PIE

Combine the chocolate chips, sugar and milk in a double boiler. Heat over simmering water until the chocolate chips melt and the sugar dissolves, stirring to blend well. Remove from the heat. Beat in the egg yolks one at a time. Add the vanilla.

Beat the egg whites in a bowl until stiff peaks form. Fold into the chocolate mixture. Spoon into the pie shell. Chill in the refrigerator for several hours. Serve with whipped cream.

If you are concerned about using raw eggs, use eggs pasteurized in their shells, which are sold at some specialty food stores, or use an equivalent amount of pasteurized egg substitute and pasteurized liquid egg whites or meringue powder.

Serves 8

1 cup (6 ounces) semisweet
    chocolate chips
2 tablespoons sugar
3 tablespoons milk
4 egg yolks
1 teaspoon vanilla extract
4 egg whites
1 baked (9-inch) pie shell, or
    1 graham cracker pie shell
Whipped cream (optional)

An IBM office products salesman commuting to work in Venice, Italy, in 1966.

CHOCOLATE MOUSSE PIE

1 tablespoon butter, softened
1 tablespoon sugar
6 ounces semisweet chocolate
3 tablespoons water
6 egg yolks
1/2 cup sugar
1 teaspoon vanilla extract
1 tablespoon rum or favorite liquor
6 egg whites
Pinch of salt

Spread the butter in a pie plate and sprinkle evenly with 1 tablespoon sugar. Shake out any excess.

Combine the chocolate with the water in a double boiler and heat over simmering water until the chocolate melts, stirring to blend well. Beat the egg yolks in a bowl, adding 1/2 cup sugar 1 tablespoon at a time and mixing well after each addition. Add the melted chocolate, vanilla and rum. Beat the egg whites with the salt in a mixing bowl until stiff peaks form. Fold into the chocolate mixture.

Spread half the filling in the prepared pie plate. Reserve the remaining filling in the refrigerator. Bake the pie in a preheated 350-degree oven for 25 minutes. Cool on a wire rack for 15 minutes. Chill in the refrigerator for 1 hour.

Spread the reserved filling over the pie. Chill the pie for 3 to 4 hours longer. Serve with whipped cream, if desired.

If you are concerned about using raw eggs, use eggs pasteurized in their shells, which are sold at some specialty food stores, or use an equivalent amount of pasteurized egg substitute and pasteurized liquid egg whites or meringue powder.

Serves 8 to 10

Employee luncheon in Stockholm, Sweden, August 15, 1933.

CHOCOLATE PEANUT BUTTER PIE

4 eggs
3/4 cup (11/2 sticks) butter, softened
11/2 cups confectioners' sugar
1 teaspoon vanilla extract
1 cup (6 ounces) semisweet
    chocolate chips or bittersweet
    chocolate chips, melted
    and cooled
1 (9-inch) graham cracker pie shell
    or baked pie shell
3/4 cup creamy peanut butter
1/4 cup (1/2 stick) butter, softened
Cream (optional)
2 cups whipped cream

Combine the eggs, 3/4 cup butter, the confectioners' sugar and vanilla in a bowl; mix until smooth with a rotary beater or the whip attachment of a standing mixer. Mix in the chocolate. Beat for 5 minutes; the mixture should be very smooth and creamy. Spoon into the pie shell.

Combine the peanut butter and 1/4 cup butter in a mixing bowl and beat until smooth. Beat in a small amount of cream if needed for the desired consistency. Spread over the pie and swirl through the two mixtures with a knife to create ribbons. Top with the whipped cream. Chill until serving time.

If you are concerned about using raw eggs, use eggs pasteurized in their shells, which are sold at some specialty food stores, or use an equivalent amount of pasteurized egg substitute.

Serves 8

CREAMY CHOCOLATE MOUSSE PIE

Mix the graham cracker crumbs with the butter in a 9-inch pie plate. Press firmly over the bottom and up the side of the plate. Bake in a preheated 375-degree oven for 6 minutes. Cool on a wire rack.

Combine the pudding mixes, milk, espresso granules and vanilla in a large bowl; whisk for 2 minutes or until smooth. Fold in the whipped topping.

Spoon the mixture into the prepared crust. Cover and chill in the refrigerator for 3 hours or longer.

Serves 10

18 chocolate graham crackers, crushed
2 tablespoons butter, melted
2 small packages sugar-free chocolate instant pudding mix
2 1/2 cups fat-free milk
1 teaspoon instant espresso granules
1 teaspoon vanilla extract
1 cup light whipped topping

TRIPLE-LAYER MUD PIE

Combine the melted chocolate with the condensed milk in a bowl and mix well. Spoon into the pie shell and sprinkle with the pecans.

Combine the pudding mixes with the milk in a large bowl. Whisk for 2 minutes or until thickened and smooth. Spoon 1 1/2 cups of the pudding over the chocolate mixture in the pie shell.

Whisk half the whipped topping into the remaining pudding. Spread over the pie and top with the remaining whipped topping. Chill in the refrigerator for 3 hours.

Serves 10

3 ounces semisweet baking chocolate, melted
1/4 cup sweetened condensed milk
1 chocolate cookie pie shell
1/2 cup chopped pecans (optional)
2 (4-ounce) packages chocolate instant pudding mix
2 cups cold milk
8 ounces whipped topping

In 1933 IBM completed construction of an engineering laboratory across North Street from the manufacturing plant in Endicott, New York.

CHOCOLATE PEANUT BUTTER COOKIE PIE

Crumble the cookie dough and press it evenly over the bottom of a 9- or 10-inch springform pan with floured fingers. Bake in a preheated 350-degree oven for 14 to 18 minutes or until golden brown. Cool in the pan on a wire rack.

Combine the confectioners' sugar, peanut butter, butter and water in a mixing bowl and beat until smooth, adding additional water if needed for the desired consistency. Mound the mixture in the prepared pie shell and press to spread evenly. Spread the melted chocolate chips over the peanut butter mixture and arrange the pecan halves over the top.

Chill until serving time. Place on a plate and remove the side of the pan. Cut into wedges to serve.

Serves 16

1 (16-ounce) roll refrigerator chocolate chip cookie dough
3 cups confectioners' sugar
1 cup peanut butter
2 tablespoons butter or margarine, softened
1/2 cup (or more) water
1 cup (6 ounces) milk chocolate chips, melted
16 pecan halves (optional)

CHOCOLATE PECAN PIE

Combine the sugar, flour, bourbon, eggs and butter in a medium bowl and mix until smooth. Stir in the chocolate chips and pecans.

Spoon the mixture into the pie shell. Bake in a preheated 350-degree oven for 50 minutes. Serve with whipped topping.

Serves 8

1 cup sugar
1/2 cup all-purpose flour
1 jigger of bourbon, or 1 teaspoon vanilla extract
2 eggs
1/2 cup (1 stick) butter or margarine, melted
1/2 cup (3 ounces) chocolate chips
1/2 to 1 cup pecans, chopped
1 unbaked pie shell

CHOCOLATE SILK PIE

1 (6-ounce) package chocolate fudge
    pudding and pie filling mix
2 cups heavy whipping cream
1 cup 2% milk
1 tablespoon instant espresso
    granules or powder
1 cup (6 ounces) semisweet
    chocolate chips
1 baked (9-inch) pie shell
8 ounces whipped topping

Combine the pudding and pie filling mix with the cream and milk in a heavy saucepan. Cook using the pudding package directions until the mixture thickens and coats the back of the spoon, stirring constantly. Remove from the heat and add the espresso granules and chocolate chips, stirring to blend well.

Spoon the mixture into the pie shell. Place plastic wrap directly on the surface of the filling to keep it from forming a skin. Chill in the refrigerator for 2 to 3 hours or until set. Top with the whipped topping to serve.

Serves 8

A farewell luncheon for Mr. and Mrs. Roy Stephens, Mr. H. Almeida T. Gomes, and Mr. Victor C. Boucas, given by the Brazilian IBM organization at the Jockey Club, Rio de Janerio, January 6, 1937.

CHOCO-BAKLAVA

Phyllo

Combine the eggs, yogurt, olive oil, vinegar, flour and 1/2 cup baking cocoa in a bowl; mix well. Knead until smooth. Cover with a slightly damp cloth and let stand for 30 minutes. Divide the dough into fifteen portions. Sift the cornstarch and 2 cups baking cocoa together. Use the mixture on a work surface to roll each dough portion into a rectangle slightly larger than a buttered 8×12-inch baking pan.

Filling

Mix the melted butter and margarine in a bowl. Layer 2 of the phyllo rectangles in the baking pan and brush with some of the butter mixture. Layer 2 more of the rectangles in the prepared pan; brush with the butter mixture and sprinkle with some of the chocolate chips and walnuts. Repeat the process twice, using all the chocolate chips and walnuts. Top with the remaining 3 rectangles and brush the top with butter. Cut the layers into small diamonds. Bake in a preheated 350-degree (180-degree C) oven for 30 minutes.

Syrup

Combine the sugar, water and lemon juice in a saucepan. Cook over low heat to form a syrup. Pour the hot syrup over the hot baklava and let stand in the pan on a wire rack until cool.

Serves 24

Phyllo
3 eggs
1/4 cup (2 ounces) plain yogurt
1/4 cup (2 ounces) olive oil
1 tablespoon (1 ounce) vinegar
2 cups (8 ounces) all-purpose flour
1/2 cup (2 ounces) baking cocoa
11/2 cups (8 ounces) cornstarch
2 cups (8 ounces) baking cocoa

Filling
1 cup plus 2 tablespoons
    (2 sticks plus 2 tablespoons/
    9 ounces) butter, melted
1 cup plus 2 tablespoons
    (2 sticks plus 2 tablespoons/
    9 ounces) margarine, melted
11/3 cups (8 ounces)
    chocolate chips
2 1/2 cups (10 ounces)
    chopped walnuts

Baklava Syrup
3 1/3 cups (27 ounces) sugar
3 1/3 cups (27 ounces) water
1 cup (8 ounces) lemon juice

CHOCOLATE COCONUT PHYLLO TRIANGLES

4 ounces semisweet chocolate
1/4 cup sweetened grated coconut, lightly toasted
1/4 cup blanched almonds, lightly toasted and chopped
1/4 cup (1/2 stick) butter, softened
6 phyllo sheets
1/4 cup (1/2 stick) butter

Process the chocolate in a food processor until finely chopped. Add the coconut, almonds and 1/4 cup butter; pulse until well mixed.

Cut the phyllo sheets into halves crosswise and stack them between two sheets of waxed paper. Cover the stack with a damp kitchen towel. Melt 1/4 cup butter in a small saucepan. Arrange one sheet of the phyllo on a work surface at a time, placing the narrow side nearest you. Brush it lightly with some of the melted butter and place a heaping tablespoon of the chocolate mixture in the upper right corner of the sheet. Fold down the top right corner to form a triangle and continue to fold the triangle over onto itself to wrap the dough completely around the filling.

Brush the triangle with some of the butter and place it on a baking sheet. Repeat the process with the remaining phyllo and filling. Bake in a preheated 400-degree oven for 8 to 12 minutes or until golden brown. Serve hot with ice cream, if desired.

You can prepare the triangles in advance, wrap well and freeze for up to 2 weeks before baking.

Serves 4 to 6

FONDANT PASTRY

Pastry

Combine the butter and flour in a mixing bowl and mix until smooth. Beat the egg yolks with the sugar in a mixing bowl. Add to the flour mixture and mix to form a dough. Knead quickly and gently. Let rest, covered, in the refrigerator for 6 hours or longer. Roll on a lightly floured surface to fit a 12-inch (30-centimeter) baking pan. Bake in a preheated 350-degree (180-degree C) oven for 15 minutes or until light brown.

Filling

Reduce the oven temperature to 250 degrees (120 degrees C). Bring the cream to a boil in a saucepan. Pour over the chocolate in a bowl and mix until the chocolate is melted and smooth. Mix in the egg. Spoon into the warm pastry shell. Bake at 250 degrees for 20 minutes or until set.

Serves 10 to 12

Pastry

1 cup (2 sticks/225 grams) butter, softened
4 1/2 cups (500 grams) all-purpose flour
9 egg yolks
1 cup minus 2 tablespoons (200 grams) castor sugar

Filling

1 cup minus 2 tablespoons (200 milliliters) cream
7 ounces (200 grams) dark chocolate
1 egg

Customer service school #262 graduation, Rio de Janerio, Brazil, April 1938.

FUDGE BROWNIE CUPS

1 (17-ounce) package frozen
    puff pastry
4 ounces unsweetened
    baking chocolate
$1/4$ cup ($1/2$ stick) butter
    or margarine
$3/4$ cup sugar
2 eggs
1 teaspoon vanilla extract
2 tablespoons all-purpose flour

Thaw the puff pastry sheets at room temperature for 30 minutes. Combine the chocolate and butter in a microwave-safe bowl. Microwave on High until the chocolate and butter melt, stirring to blend well. Stir in the sugar, eggs and vanilla. Add the flour and mix well.

Unfold each pastry sheet on a lightly floured surface and roll each into a 12×15-inch rectangle. Cut into twenty 3-inch squares. Press each square into a muffin cup. Spoon 1 tablespoon of the chocolate mixture into each prepared muffin cup. Bake in a preheated 400-degree oven for 15 to 20 minutes or until the pastry is golden brown. Cool in the muffin cups on a wire rack.

Makes 20

An IBM typewriter tape punch, type 884, travels by river to a coal mining customer in Vietnam, 1961.

WHITE CHOCOLATE MOUSSE PASTRIES

Bake the pastry shells using the package directions; cool on a wire rack. Combine 1/4 cup cream with the white chocolate in a microwave-safe bowl. Microwave on High for 2 minutes or until the white chocolate is almost melted; stir to blend well. Let cool for 20 minutes or to room temperature.

Beat 1/4 cup cream at medium speed in a mixing bowl until soft peaks form. Fold into the white chocolate mixture one-half at a time. Spoon into the pastry shells. Drizzle with the semisweet chocolate. Chill for up to 6 hours before serving.

Serves 6

1 (10-ounce) package frozen puff
   pastry shells
1/4 cup heavy whipping cream
6 ounces white chocolate
1/4 cup heavy whipping cream
1 ounce semisweet chocolate, melted

This 1980 view of St. Mark's Square in Venice perhaps proves two old adages: the first, said by veteran employees, "In IBM even the 'wild ducks' fly in formation," the other, said by just about everyone, "Birds of a feather flock together."

pies & pastries 133

desserts

THINK signs rendered in a variety of languages for display by IBM employees around the world.

PUBLIC RELATIONS

The eight-bar logo. THINK. Cutting-edge products. Barrier-breaking

corporate policies. IBM's public face and reputation have always been

part of what makes the company a leader. From its advertisements and

graphically interesting logos to the technology from its labs and

corporate policies from its headquarters, IBM has never been afraid to

be in the public spotlight.

Coconut Chocolate Almond Cheesecake 138

Fudge Truffle Cheesecake 139

Killer Chocolate Cheesecake 140

Chocolate Mint Swirl Cheesecake with Chocolate Nut Crust 141

Chocolate Peppermint Cheesecake 142

Triple Chocolate Cheesecake 143

Chocolate Zebra Cheesecake 144

Butterfinger Dessert 145

Cream Puff Dessert 145

Devil's Float 146

Girdle Buster 146

Mexican Chocolate Icebox Dessert 147

Grandma's Icebox Dessert 148

Chocolate Mess 148

Meringue Filled with Chocolate and Nuts 149

Chocolate Mousse with Frangelico 150

Dark and White Chocolate Mousse 150

Three-Chocolate Ice Cream Mousse 152

Healthy Chocolate Mousse 153

Manitoba "Moose" Chocolate Pudding 153

Four-Three-Two-One Chocolate Pudding 155

Chocolate Pudding Trifle 155

Chocolate Kahlua Trifle 156

Chocolate Trifle 156

Brownie Trifle 158

Chocolate Meltdown 158

Creepy Mud Dessert 159

Chocolate Gravy 159

Chocolate Sauce 160

Hot Fudge Sauce 160

Fudge Syrup 160

COCONUT CHOCOLATE
ALMOND CHEESECAKE

Chocolate Cookie Crust

1¹/2 cups chocolate wafer cookie
    crumbs (28 to 30 cookies)
3 tablespoons sugar
¹/4 cup (¹/2 stick) butter or
    margarine, melted

Cheesecake

32 ounces cream cheese, softened
1 cup sugar
3 eggs
1 (14-ounce) package
    flaked coconut
2 cups (12 ounces) milk
    chocolate chips
¹/2 cup slivered almonds, toasted
1 teaspoon vanilla extract
¹/2 cup (3 ounces) semisweet
    chocolate chips
Chopped toasted almonds,
    for garnish

Crust

Combine the cookie crumbs, sugar and butter in a bowl and mix well.
Press over the bottom of a 10-inch springform pan.

Cheesecake

Combine the cream cheese, sugar and eggs in a mixing bowl and
beat at medium speed until light and fluffy. Stir in the coconut, milk
chocolate chips, ¹/2 cup almonds and the vanilla. Spoon the mixture
into the prepared crust. Bake in a preheated 350-degree oven for
1 hour. Cool on a wire rack.

Place the semisweet chocolate chips in a sealable plastic bag.
Submerge the bag in warm water and let stand until the chocolate
chips melt. Snip a tiny corner off the bag and drizzle the chocolate
over the cheesecake. Garnish with toasted almonds. Chill, covered,
for 8 hours. Place on a serving plate and remove the side of the pan.

Serves 10 to 12

FUDGE TRUFFLE CHEESECAKE

Crust

Combine the vanilla wafer crumbs, confectioners' sugar, baking cocoa and butter in a medium bowl and mix well. Press firmly over the bottom of a 9-inch springform pan.

Cheesecake

Melt the chocolate chips in a heavy saucepan over very low heat. Beat the cream cheese in a mixing bowl until light and fluffy. Add the condensed milk and beat until smooth. Add the melted chocolate, eggs and vanilla and mix well.

Spoon the mixture into the prepared crust. Bake in a preheated 300-degree oven for 1 hour and 5 minutes or until the center is set. Let cool on a wire rack and place in the refrigerator to chill. Place on a serving plate and remove the side of the pan.

Serves 12

Vanilla Wafer Crust

1¹/2 cups vanilla wafer crumbs
¹/2 cup confectioners' sugar
¹/3 cup baking cocoa
¹/3 cup butter or margarine, melted

Cheesecake

2 cups (12 ounces) semisweet
    chocolate chips
24 ounces cream cheese, softened
1 (14-ounce) can sweetened
    condensed milk
4 eggs
2 teaspoons vanilla extract

仲間に「野鴨」がいるのは
タノシイものです

IBM
日本アイ・ビー・エム株式会社 東京都千代田区永田町1-14

The "wild duck" that Tom Watson, Jr., hailed as a symbol of independent thinking is featured in this 1967 Japanese newspaper ad with this headline: "It is fun to work with wild ducks." Watson was drawn to the analogy in a story by Søren Kierkegaard, the Danish philosopher.

KILLER CHOCOLATE CHEESECAKE

Chocolate Crumb Crust

2 cups chocolate cookie crumbs

6 tablespoons (3/4 stick) unsalted butter, melted

Cheesecake

16 ounces bittersweet chocolate or semisweet chocolate, chopped

1/4 cup (1/2 stick) unsalted butter

2 tablespoons baking cocoa

24 ounces cream cheese, softened

1 cup sugar

4 eggs

Pinch of salt

1 1/2 cups sour cream, at room temperature

2 teaspoons vanilla extract

Crust

Butter a 9-inch springform pan and wrap the outside tightly with heavy-duty foil. Mix the cookie crumbs and butter in a bowl. Press over the bottom of the prepared pan. Bake in a preheated 350-degree oven for 8 to 10 minutes.

Cheesecake

Place the chocolate and butter in a heatproof bowl. Place over a saucepan of simmering water and heat until the chocolate and butter melt, whisking until smooth. Whisk in the baking cocoa. Let cool for 20 minutes.

Beat the cream cheese and sugar in a large mixing bowl until light and fluffy. Beat in the eggs one at a time. Add the chocolate mixture and salt and mix just until smooth. Add the sour cream and vanilla; mix well.

Spoon the mixture into the prepared crust. Place the springform pan in a larger roasting pan and place on the center oven rack. Add enough boiling water to the larger pan to reach halfway up the side of the springform pan. Bake in the preheated 350-degree oven for 45 to 50 minutes or until the center is almost set; do not overbake. Remove from the oven and let cool in the water bath for 15 minutes.

Remove the springform pan to a wire rack to cool completely. Remove the foil and chill, loosely covered, for 12 hours or longer. Let stand at room temperature for 20 minutes. Place on a serving plate and remove the side of the pan. Smooth the side of the cheesecake with a knife.

Serves 12 to 16

CHOCOLATE MINT SWIRL CHEESECAKE WITH CHOCOLATE NUT CRUST

Crust

Combine the walnuts, chocolate, sugar and butter in a bowl and mix well. Press over the bottom of a 9-inch springform pan sprayed with nonstick cooking spray. Chill for 1 hour or longer.

Cheesecake

Beat the egg whites in a mixing bowl until stiff peaks form. Blend the chocolate with the peppermint schnapps in a double boiler and heat over simmering water until the chocolate melts.

Combine the cream cheese, sour cream, sugar, chestnut flour, vanilla and salt in a mixing bowl; beat until smooth. Beat in the egg yolks one at a time. Fold in the egg whites. Swirl in the chocolate mixture with a knife.

Spoon the mixture into the prepared crust. Bake in a preheated 350-degree oven for 1 hour. Turn off the oven and let the cheesecake cool in the oven with the door ajar for 1 hour. Chill in the refrigerator. Place on a serving plate and remove the side of the pan. Serve with whipped cream, if desired.

Serves 8 to 10

Chocolate Nut Crust

1 1/2 cups ground walnuts

4 ounces semisweet chocolate, melted

1/2 cup sugar

1/3 cup unsalted butter, melted

Cheesecake

4 egg whites

4 ounces semisweet chocolate

2 tablespoons peppermint schnapps

24 ounces cream cheese, softened

1 cup sour cream

3/4 cup sugar

2 tablespoons chestnut flour

1 1/2 teaspoons vanilla extract

1 teaspoon salt

4 egg yolks

CHOCOLATE PEPPERMINT CHEESECAKE

Chocolate Wafer Crust

1 cup chocolate wafer crumbs

3 tablespoons margarine, melted

Cheesecake

1 envelope unflavored gelatin

1/4 cup cold water

16 ounces cream cheese, softened

1/2 cup sugar

1/2 cup milk

1/4 cup crushed peppermint candy

1 cup heavy whipping cream,
    whipped

1 (3-ounce) milk chocolate candy
    bar, finely chopped

Whipped cream, crushed
    peppermint candy and
    chocolate curls, for garnish

Crust

Mix the cookie crumbs with the margarine in a bowl. Press over the bottom of a 9-inch springform pan. Bake in a preheated 350-degree oven for 10 minutes. Cool on a wire rack.

Cheesecake

Sprinkle the gelatin over the cold water in a small saucepan; let stand until softened. Heat over low heat, stirring until the gelatin dissolves completely. Beat the cream cheese with the sugar at medium speed in a mixing bowl until light and fluffy. Add the gelatin, milk and 1/4 cup peppermint candy gradually, mixing constantly. Chill until slightly thickened but not set.

Fold in 1 cup whipped cream and the chopped chocolate. Spoon into the prepared crust. Chill until firm. Place on a serving plate and remove the side of the pan. Garnish with additional whipped cream, crushed peppermint and chocolate curls.

Serves 10

TRIPLE CHOCOLATE CHEESECAKE

Crust

Combine the chocolate wafers and brown sugar in a food processor and process for 2 minutes. Mix with the butter in a bowl. Press the mixture over the bottom and up the side of a 9-inch springform pan. Bake in a preheated 325-degree oven for 10 minutes. Cool on a wire rack.

Cheesecake

Combine the cream cheese, sour cream and brown sugar in a mixing bowl and beat at medium-high speed for 2 minutes. Add the eggs and beat for 2 minutes. Stir in the flour and vanilla.

Microwave the chocolate in a microwave-safe bowl for 1 minute or until melted, stirring twice. Fold 1/2 cup of the cream cheese mixture into the chocolate; then fold the chocolate into the remaining cream cheese mixture.

Spoon the mixture into the prepared crust. Bake in a preheated 325-degree oven for 1 hour and 10 minutes. Turn off the oven and let the cheesecake stand in the oven with the door ajar for 1 hour.

Topping

Bring the cream to a boil in a small saucepan over medium heat. Pour over the chocolate in a heatproof bowl and stir until the chocolate melts and is well blended. Spread over the cheesecake. Chill in the refrigerator. Place on a serving plate and remove the side of the pan. Garnish with white chocolate curls and strawberries.

Serves 12

Chocolate Butter Crust

9 ounces chocolate wafers or
    chocolate graham crackers
1/4 cup packed brown sugar
6 tablespoons (3/4 stick) lightly
    salted butter, melted

Cheesecake

32 ounces cream cheese, softened
1 cup sour cream
3/4 cup packed brown sugar
4 eggs
3 tablespoons all-purpose flour
1 teaspoon vanilla extract
10 ounces bittersweet chocolate,
    chopped

Topping

1/4 cup heavy cream
2 ounces bittersweet chocolate,
    chopped
White chocolate curls and
    strawberries, for garnish

CHOCOLATE ZEBRA CHEESECAKE

Chocolate Chip Crust

1 1/2 cups chocolate wafer crumbs
    (about 30 wafers)
3 tablespoons butter or margarine,
    melted
1/2 cup (3 ounces) semisweet
    chocolate chips

Cheesecake

1 1/4 cups sugar
3 tablespoons cornstarch
1/4 teaspoon salt
32 ounces cream cheese, softened
5 eggs
1 cup sour cream
1 cup heavy cream
2 teaspoons vanilla extract
8 ounces semisweet chocolate
8 ounces white chocolate

Topping

1/2 cup heavy cream
4 ounces semisweet chocolate
Whipped cream and maraschino
    cherries or mint, for garnish

Crust

Mix the cookie crumbs and butter in a bowl. Press over the bottom of a greased 9-inch springform pan. Bake in a preheated 350-degree oven for 12 to 15 minutes or until firm. Remove from the oven and sprinkle with the chocolate chips. Let stand until the chocolate chips melt and spread evenly over the crust. Chill in the refrigerator.

Cheesecake

Mix the sugar, cornstarch and salt in a small bowl. Beat the cream cheese at medium speed in a large mixing bowl until light and fluffy. Add the sugar mixture gradually, beating constantly. Beat in the eggs, sour cream, heavy cream and vanilla at low speed. Divide the mixture evenly between two containers with pouring spouts. Melt the semisweet chocolate in a small saucepan over low heat. Pour the chocolate into one of the containers. Melt the white chocolate in a small saucepan over low heat. Pour into the second container. Pour half the dark batter into the center of the prepared crust; do not spread the batter. Hold the container with the white batter about 2 feet above the springform pan and pour about half the batter into the center of the dark batter; pouring from this height will force the batter in the center of the pan toward the edge of the pan and form a bull's-eye design. Repeat the procedure three times, decreasing the amount of batter each time and continuing to pour from the same height; end with the white batter. The top of the cheesecake should appear to be a series of concentric circles. Bake the cheesecake in a preheated 350-degree oven for 30 minutes. Reduce the oven temperature to 225 degrees and bake for 1 3/4 hours longer or until the center is set. Turn off the oven and let the cheesecake stand in the oven for 1 hour. Loosen the cheesecake from the side of the pan with a thin spatula and cool in the pan on a wire rack. Chill for 8 hours or longer. Place on a serving plate and remove the side of the pan.

Topping

Heat the cream in a 1-quart saucepan over medium heat until small bubbles form around the edge; remove from the heat. Add the chocolate and stir until melted and smooth. Cool for 10 minutes. Spread over the cheesecake. Chill for 30 to 45 minutes or until the topping is set. Garnish with whipped cream and maraschino cherries or mint.

Serves 12 to 16

BUTTERFINGER DESSERT

Combine the graham cracker crumbs, crushed candy bars and margarine in a bowl and mix well. Press half the mixture into a 9×13-inch dish.

Combine the pudding mixes and milk in a mixing bowl and mix until thickened and smooth. Add the ice cream and mix well. Spread in the prepared dish and chill until set. Spread the whipped topping over the top and sprinkle with the remaining crumb mixture. Chill until serving time.

Serves 12

2 cups chocolate graham
    cracker crumbs
4 Butterfinger candy bars, crushed
1/2 cup (1 stick) margarine, melted
2 (4-ounce) packages vanilla instant
    pudding mix
2 cups milk
1 quart vanilla ice cream, softened
8 ounces whipped topping

CREAM PUFF DESSERT

Combine the butter and water in a saucepan. Bring to a boil over medium heat. Add the flour all at once, stirring until the mixture forms a ball and leaves the side of the saucepan. Remove from the heat and let stand for 5 minutes. Beat in the eggs one at a time.

Spread the mixture in a greased 9×13-inch baking pan. Bake in a preheated 400-degree oven for 30 to 35 minutes or until puffed and golden brown. Cool in the pan on a wire rack.

Combine the cream cheese, milk and pudding mixes in a mixing bowl and beat until smooth. Spread over the baked layer. Chill in the refrigerator for 20 minutes. Spread the whipped topping over the top and chill until serving time. Drizzle with chocolate syrup and caramel syrup and sprinkle with the almonds and coconut to serve.

Serves 12

1 cup (2 sticks) butter
1 cup water
1 cup all-purpose flour
4 eggs
8 ounces cream cheese, softened
3 cups cold milk
2 (4-ounce) packages chocolate
    instant pudding mix
8 ounces whipped topping
Chocolate syrup
Caramel syrup
1/2 cup chopped toasted almonds
1/2 cup toasted flaked coconut

DEVIL'S FLOAT

1 cup sugar
2 cups water
2 tablespoons butter, softened
1/2 cup sugar
1/2 cup milk
1 cup all-purpose flour
1 teaspoon baking powder
3 tablespoons baking cocoa
1/2 teaspoon salt
1 cup nuts

Combine 1 cup sugar with the water in a saucepan. Bring to a boil and boil for 10 minutes. Pour into a 9×9-inch baking pan.

Cream the butter and 1/2 cup sugar in a mixing bowl until light and fluffy. Add the milk, flour, baking powder, baking cocoa, salt and nuts; mix well. Drop the batter by spoonfuls into the hot sugar syrup. Bake in a preheated 375-degree oven for 45 minutes.

Serves 6

GIRDLE BUSTER

1 cup all-purpose flour
1/2 cup (1 stick) butter, melted
1 cup pecans, chopped
8 ounces cream cheese, softened
1 cup confectioners' sugar
1 cup whipped topping
1 (6-ounce) package chocolate
    instant pudding mix
3 cups milk
8 ounces whipped topping
1 cup chopped toasted pecans

Combine the flour, butter and 1 cup pecans in a bowl and mix well. Press into an 8×11-inch baking dish. Bake in a preheated 350-degree oven for 15 minutes or until brown. Let cool to room temperature.

Combine the cream cheese, confectioners' sugar and 1 cup whipped topping in a bowl and mix until smooth. Spread over the cooled baked layer.

Combine the pudding mix with the milk in a bowl and beat until thickened and smooth. Spread over the cream cheese layer. Spread 8 ounces whipped topping over the layers and sprinkle with 1 cup toasted pecans. Chill for 8 hours or longer.

Serves 12

MEXICAN CHOCOLATE ICEBOX DESSERT

Line the bottom and side of a 9-inch springform pan with some of the ladyfingers, placing the rounded sides toward the outside of the pan. Combine 3/4 cup cream with the granulated sugar and baking chocolate in a small heavy saucepan. Heat over low heat until the chocolate melts, stirring until smooth. Let cool to room temperature.

Combine 1 cup confectioners' sugar with the butter and 1 teaspoon vanilla in a large mixing bowl; beat until smooth. Beat in the cooled chocolate mixture.

Combine 2 cups cream, 2 tablespoons confectioners' sugar, 1 teaspoon vanilla and the cinnamon in a large mixing bowl. Beat with clean dry beaters until firm peaks form. Fold half the whipped cream into the chocolate mixture. Spread half the chocolate mixture in the prepared springform pan.

Arrange a layer of ladyfingers over the chocolate filling and spread the remaining chocolate filling over the ladyfingers. Pipe or spread the remaining whipped cream over the filling and sprinkle with the grated chocolate. Chill, covered, for 3 to 24 hours. Place on a serving plate and remove the side of the pan.

Serves 12

60 ladyfingers
3/4 cup heavy cream
1/4 cup granulated sugar
4 ounces unsweetened baking chocolate, chopped
1 cup confectioners' sugar
1/2 cup (1 stick) unsalted butter, softened
1 teaspoon vanilla extract
2 cups heavy whipping cream, chilled
2 tablespoons confectioners' sugar
1 teaspoon vanilla extract
1 teaspoon ground cinnamon
1 ounce semisweet chocolate, grated

GRANDMA'S ICEBOX DESSERT

1 package graham crackers
Milk
1 (6-ounce) package chocolate
    pudding and pie filling mix
2 to 3 bananas, sliced
2 cups heavy whipping cream
1 tablespoon sugar
1 teaspoon vanilla extract

Arrange some of the graham crackers in a 9×13-inch dish; sprinkle with a small amount of milk. Prepare and cook the pudding mix using the package directions. Spoon the hot pudding over the graham crackers. Add a second layer of graham crackers over the pudding and sprinkle with a small amount of milk. Arrange the bananas over the graham crackers. Top with a third layer of graham crackers and sprinkle with milk. Chill in the refrigerator.

Combine the cream with the sugar and vanilla in a mixing bowl; beat until firm peaks form. Spread over the layers. Chill for 30 to 45 minutes longer.

Serves 10

CHOCOLATE MESS

1 (2-layer) package chocolate
    cake mix
1 (4-ounce) package chocolate
    instant pudding mix
4 eggs
1 cup water
2 cups sour cream
3/4 cup vegetable oil
1 cup (6 ounces) chocolate chips

Whisk the cake mix with the pudding mix in a large bowl. Beat the eggs with the water in a medium bowl. Add the sour cream and oil and beat until smooth. Add to the mixes and mix well. Stir in the chocolate chips.

Spoon the pudding mixture into a slow cooker sprayed with nonstick cooking spray. Cook on Low for 6 to 8 hours or until the top springs back when lightly touched. Serve in bowls with ice cream.

Serves 8 to 10

MERINGUE FILLED WITH CHOCOLATE AND NUTS

Meringue

Combine the egg whites with the baking powder and salt in a bowl; beat until soft peaks form. Add the sugar 1 teaspoon at a time, beating constantly. Add the vanilla and beat at high speed until stiff peaks form. Spread part of the mixture in a 6- or 7-inch circle on a baking sheet lined with baking parchment. Spoon the remaining egg white mixture around the base circle, building it up to form a bowl.

Bake in a preheated 275-degree oven for 1 hour. Turn off the oven and let stand in the oven for 1 hour. Remove from the baking parchment to a round platter.

Filling

Beat the egg yolks with 1/2 cup sugar in a bowl. Soften the gelatin in 1/3 cup water in a saucepan. Bring to a boil, stirring to dissolve the gelatin completely. Add the egg yolk mixture, stirring constantly. Combine the chocolate with 1/2 cup water and 1/4 cup sugar in a microwave-safe bowl. Microwave until the chocolate melts, stirring to blend well. Add to the egg yolk mixture, mixing well. Let stand until cool.

Add the cream and liqueur to the filling and beat until smooth. Stir in pecans. Spoon into the meringue and chill for 3 to 4 hours. You can also top with chantilly cream and/or strawberries.

Serves 12

Meringue

3 egg whites
1/2 teaspoon baking powder
1/8 teaspoon salt
1 cup sugar
1 teaspoon vanilla extract

Chocolate Filling

3 egg yolks
1/2 cup sugar
1 envelope unflavored gelatin
1/3 cup water
3 ounces dark chocolate or
    bittersweet chocolate
1/2 cup water
1/4 cup sugar
1/2 cup cream
1/4 cup coffee liqueur
Pecans or other nuts

CHOCOLATE MOUSSE WITH FRANGELICO

4 egg whites
Pinch of sea salt
Pinch of cream of tartar (optional)
4 ounces semisweet chocolate or
    dark chocolate, chopped
2 tablespoons Frangelico or
    other hazelnut liqueur
1/4 cup (1/2 stick) butter, cut into
    1/2-tablespoon slices
4 egg yolks

Combine the egg whites with the sea salt and cream of tartar in a bowl and beat with a hand mixer until stiff peaks form; the egg whites are ready if they do not fall out of the bowl when it is inverted.

Place the chocolate in a heavy pan and heat in a preheated 200-degree oven until melted. Remove from the oven and stir in the liqueur. Add the butter and beat until smooth. Beat in the egg yolks one at a time. Return to the oven and heat for 2 minutes. Fold the egg whites gently into the mousse. Spoon into serving dishes or stemmed glasses. Chill for 2 hours or longer.

If you are concerned about using raw eggs, use eggs pasteurized in their shells, which are sold at some specialty food stores, or use an equivalent amount of pasteurized egg substitute.

Serves 4

DARK AND WHITE CHOCOLATE MOUSSE

2 teaspoons unflavored gelatin
2 tablespoons cold water
10 ounces dark chocolate
12 ounces white chocolate
2 (14-ounce) cans sweetened
    condensed milk
6 egg whites
6 tablespoons sugar

Soften the gelatin in the cold water in a cup. Place the dark chocolate and white chocolate in separate microwave-safe bowls. Add 1 can of condensed milk to each bowl. Microwave both mixtures on High until the chocolates melt, stirring to blend well. Let stand, covered with plastic wrap, for 1 hour. Beat the egg whites and sugar in a mixing bowl until stiff peaks form. Fold half the egg whites into each of the chocolate mixtures with a spatula. Fold the gelatin mixture into the white chocolate mixture. Spoon the white chocolate mousse onto a platter. Add the dark chocolate mousse gradually, swirling to marbleize. Cover with plastic wrap and chill for 8 hours.

If you are concerned about using raw egg whites, use eggs pasteurized in their shells, which are sold at some specialty food stores, or an equivalent amount of pasteurized liquid egg whites or meringue powder.

Serves 10

The IBM Pavilion at the 1964–1965 New York World's Fair covered 54,038 square feet (1.2 acres) in Flushing Meadow, New York. Designed by Charles Eames and Eero Saarinen Associates, the pavilion created the effect of a covered garden, with all exhibits in the open beneath a grove of forty-five 32-foot-high, man-made steel trees. The pavilion was divided into six sections: The "Information Machine," a 90-foot-high main theater with multiple screen projection; pentagon theaters, where puppet-like devices explained the workings of data processing systems; computer application area; probability machine; scholar's walk; and a 4,500-square-foot administration building.

THREE-CHOCOLATE ICE CREAM MOUSSE
(SEMIFREDDO AI TRE CIOCCOLATI)

Mousse

4 ounces (125 grams)
  dark chocolate
5 ounces (150 grams)
  white chocolate
5 ounces (150 grams) nougat
  chocolate or milk chocolate
5 tablespoons (150 milliliters)
  heavy cream
6 egg yolks
1/2 cup plus 2 tablespoons
  (1 1/4 sticks/135 grams)
  butter, softened
6 egg whites
3 tablespoons sugar
2 tablespoons almond oil or
  cornflower oil

Strawberry Sauce

1 1/4 pounds (600 grams)
  strawberries or raspberries
2 tablespoons confectioners' sugar
3 tablespoons fruit schnapps
Mint leaves, for garnish

Mousse

Chop the dark chocolate and place in a double boiler or microwave-safe bowl. Heat over simmering water or in the microwave until melted. Repeat the process with the white chocolate and the nougat chocolate, keeping each chocolate in separate bowls. Bring the cream to a boil in a saucepan. Pour one-third of the cream over each chocolate and stir to blend well. Let stand until cool.

Add 2 egg yolks and one-third of the butter to each chocolate and whisk until smooth. Whisk the egg whites with the sugar in a large bowl; add the almond oil and whisk until stiff peaks form. Fold one-third of the mixture into each chocolate.

Oil a 4×12-inch (10×30-centimeter) mold lightly and line it with baking parchment. Cut a piece of baking parchment to fit the top. Spread the dark chocolate mixture in the prepared mold. Place in the refrigerator or freezer for 10 minutes. Spread the white chocolate mixture carefully over the dark and place in the refrigerator or freezer for 10 minutes. Spread the nougat chocolate mixture evenly over the top.

Cover with the prepared baking parchment and plastic wrap. Chill in the refrigerator for 6 hours or longer or freeze until serving time. Unmold onto a serving plate and cut into slices.

Sauce

Combine the strawberries with the confectioners' sugar and fruit schnapps in a blender. Process until smooth. Spoon over the slices of mousse and garnish with mint leaves.

If you are concerned about using raw eggs, use eggs pasteurized in their shells, which are sold at some specialty food stores, or use an equivalent amount of pasteurized egg substitute.

Serves 8 to 10

HEALTHY CHOCOLATE MOUSSE

Place the chocolate chips in a double boiler or microwave-safe bowl. Melt over simmering water or microwave on High for 1 to 3 minutes or until melted, stirring frequently.

Beat the tofu at high speed in a mixing bowl until very smooth. Fold in the chocolate. Spoon into four dessert cups and chill for 30 minutes or longer. Garnish with whipped cream and shaved chocolate.

Serves 4

1 cup (6 ounces) milk chocolate chips or semisweet chocolate chips
16 ounces dessert-style silken tofu, drained
Whipped cream and shaved chocolate, for garnish

MANITOBA "MOOSE" CHOCOLATE PUDDING

Combine the sugar with 2 cups milk in a saucepan. Heat over medium heat until steaming. Whisk the baking cocoa with the cornstarch in a large bowl. Whisk in the eggs and 1/2 cup milk. Whisk half the hot milk into the egg mixture; then whisk the egg mixture back into the saucepan gradually. Cook over medium-low heat for 5 minutes or until thickened to pudding consistency, whisking constantly. Add 1 cup chocolate chips and stir until the chips melt.

Spoon into six to eight dessert cups or a large serving bowl; use long-stem glasses or martini glasses for special occasions. Sprinkle with the pecans, 1/4 cup chocolate chips and the miniature marshmallows.

You can vary the mousse by the addition of other ingredients. For Mocha Pudding, *add 1 tablespoon instant coffee granules and 1 tablespoon brandy or rum. For* Chocolate Mint Pudding, *add 1 teaspoon or more mint extract. For* Chocolate Orange Pudding, *add 3 tablespoons orange juice concentrate and the finely grated zest of 1 orange.*

Serves 6 to 8

1/3 cup sugar
2 cups milk
1/3 cup baking cocoa
3 tablespoons cornstarch
2 eggs
1/2 cup milk
1 cup (6 ounces) semisweet chocolate chips
1/2 cup toasted pecans, hazelnuts or walnuts (optional)
1/4 cup semisweet chocolate chips (optional)
1/2 cup miniature marshmallows (optional)

Italian convention banquet, Milan, Italy, April 28, 1938.

FOUR-THREE-TWO-ONE CHOCOLATE PUDDING

Mix the sugar and cornstarch in a microwave-safe bowl. Add the milk and baking cocoa and mix until smooth.

Microwave on High for 1 minute; stir. Repeat the process until the mixture comes to a boil. Stir in the butter until melted.

Serves 2 to 4

$1/4$ cup sugar, or to taste
3 tablespoons cornstarch
2 cups milk
1 tablespoon baking cocoa
1 tablespoon butter

CHOCOLATE PUDDING TRIFLE

Prepare and bake the cake mix using the package directions. Let cool for 30 minutes. Tear the cake into small pieces in a large bowl. Beat the pudding mixes and milk in a large bowl at medium speed for 3 minutes. Chill, uncovered, in the refrigerator for 15 minutes. Combine the cream with the sugar and vanilla in a medium bowl. Beat until soft peaks form.

Reserve a small amount of the cake pieces and crumble into fine crumbs. Layer the remaining cake pieces, the chocolate pudding mixture and the whipped cream mixture one-third at a time in a large glass bowl. Top with the cake crumbs. Chill for 2 hours or longer before serving.

Serves 8

1 (2-layer) package chocolate
   cake mix
2 (4-ounce) packages chocolate
   instant pudding mix
3 cups milk
2 cups heavy whipping cream
$1^1/2$ tablespoons sugar
2 teaspoons vanilla extract

CHOCOLATE KAHLUA TRIFLE

1 (2-layer) package devil's food
    cake mix
2 (4-ounce) packages chocolate
    instant pudding mix
2 cups heavy whipping cream
3 tablespoons sugar
2 tablespoons amaretto, or
    2 teaspoons vanilla extract
1 cup Kahlúa
2 Heath candy bars, chopped

Prepare and bake the cake mix using the package directions for a
9×13-inch cake pan. Let the cake cool completely in the pan and cut
into cubes. Prepare the pudding mixes using the package directions.
Combine the cream with the sugar in a bowl and beat until soft peaks
form. Add the amaretto and beat until firm peaks form.

Arrange half the cake cubes in a large bowl. Drizzle half the Kahlúa
evenly over the cake cubes. Spread with half the pudding mixture and
half the whipped cream mixture. Sprinkle half the chopped candy
over the top. Repeat the layers. Chill, covered, for 4 hours or longer.

You can substitute whipped topping for the amaretto whipped cream.

Serves 10

CHOCOLATE TRIFLE

1 (2-layer) package dark chocolate
    cake mix or chocolate fudge
    cake mix
1 (6-ounce) package chocolate
    instant pudding mix
1/2 cup brewed coffee (optional)
12 ounces (or more)
    whipped topping
2 cups (12 ounces) English
    toffee bits

Prepare and bake the cake mix using the package directions. Let cool
in the pan. Prepare the pudding mix using the package directions.
Crumble the cake and spread almost half the crumbs in a 4 1/2- or
5-quart glass bowl.

Drizzle half the coffee over the cake and spread with half the pudding
and half the whipped topping. Sprinkle with half the toffee bits.

Reserve 1/2 cup of the remaining cake and a few toffee bits.
Repeat the layers and top with the reserved cake and toffee bits.
Chill, covered, for 4 to 24 hours before serving; longer chilling time
improves the flavor.

Serves 12 to 15

"EVER ONWARD"

(I. B. M. Rally Song, written especially for the
International Business Machines Corporation)

There's a thrill in store for all,
For we're about to toast
The corporation that we represent.
We're here to cheer each pioneer
And also proudly boast
Of that "man of men," our sterling president.
The name of T. J. Watson means a courage none can stem:
And we feel honored to be here to toast the "I. B. M.".

Chorus

EVER ONWARD — EVER ONWARD !
That's the spirit that has brought us fame!
We're big, but bigger we will be:
We can't fail for all can see
That to serve humanity has been our aim!
Our products now are known in every zone,
Our reputation sparkles like a gem!
We've fought our way through—and new
Fields we're sure to conquer too
For the EVER ONWARD I. B. M.

Second Chorus

EVER ONWARD — EVER ONWARD !
We're bound for the top to never fall!
Right here and now we thankfully
Pledge sincerest loyalty
To the corporation that's the best of all!
Our leaders we revere, and while we're here
Let's show the world just what we think of them!
So let us sing, men! SING, MEN !
Once or twice then sing again
For the EVER ONWARD I. B. M.

*The IBM rally song, "Ever Onward," was written in
1931 by IBMer Fred Tappe. This rousing number was only one
of many songs written and sung by the company's
marketing representatives, students, managers, and employees
whenever they gathered for group meetings.*

BROWNIE TRIFLE

1 recipe favorite brownie mix, prepared
1/2 cup Kahlúa or very strong brewed coffee
2 (6-ounce) packages chocolate instant pudding mix
4 cups milk
12 ounces whipped topping
6 (11/2-ounce) Heath candy bars, crushed in a plastic bag

Poke holes in the warm brownies with the end of a wooden spoon. Brush with the Kahlúa and let stand for 5 minutes. Crumble the brownies. Prepare the pudding mixes with the milk in a bowl; do not chill the pudding.

Layer the crumbled brownies, pudding, whipped topping and candy bars one-third at a time in a 3-quart trifle bowl. Chill, covered, for 8 hours.

Serves 10 to 12

CHOCOLATE MELTDOWN

3/4 cup semisweet chocolate chips or raspberry swirl chocolate chips
1/2 cup (1 stick) butter
2 eggs
3 tablespoons all-purpose flour
3/4 cup superfine sugar or granulated sugar
1/2 cup (3 ounces) white chocolate chips

Melt the semisweet chocolate chips with the butter in a double boiler over simmering water. Let cool to room temperature. Combine the eggs, flour and sugar in a bowl and beat until smooth. Add the melted chocolate mixture and mix well. Fold in the white chocolate chips.

Spoon into four buttered 2/3-cup ramekins and place on a baking sheet. Bake in a preheated 400-degree oven for 20 minutes or until the tops are cracked and shiny and the insides are hot and gooey. Serve warm, using caution to handle the ramekins.

Serves 4

CREEPY MUD DESSERT

Combine the pudding mixes and milk in a mixing bowl and whisk for 3 minutes or until smooth. Stir in the whipped topping. Fold in half the cookie crumbs and half the gummy worms.

Spoon the pudding mixture into a 9×13-inch dish and sprinkle with the remaining cookie crumbs. Chill for 1 hour or longer. Arrange the remaining gummy worms over the dessert to appear as if they are crawling out of the dessert.

Serves 12 to 15

2 (4-ounce) packages chocolate
   instant pudding mix
3 1/2 cups cold milk
12 ounces whipped topping
1 (16-ounce) package chocolate
   sandwich cookies, crushed
1 1/2 cups gummy worms

CHOCOLATE GRAVY

Mix the sugar and baking cocoa in a small bowl. Melt the margarine in a skillet over medium heat. Stir in the flour until smooth. Add the baking cocoa mixture and mix well.

Cook until smooth, stirring constantly. Add milk gradually until of the desired consistency, whisking constantly. Cook until smooth and thickened, whisking constantly. Stir in the vanilla. Serve alone or with biscuits.

Serves 4

1/2 cup sugar
1/4 cup baking cocoa
1/2 cup (1 stick) margarine
5 tablespoons all-purpose flour
Milk
1 teaspoon vanilla extract

CHOCOLATE SAUCE

1 package chocolate pudding and
    pie filling mix
2 cups milk
2 cups brewed instant coffee, or
    1 cup brewed coffee and
    1 cup water

Combine the pudding and pie filling mix with the milk in a saucepan. Cook using the pudding package directions. Add the coffee and cook until heat through and smooth, stirring constantly.

Serves 6

HOT FUDGE SAUCE

1¹/2 cups sugar
1 tablespoon cornstarch
Pinch of salt
4 ounces unsweetened
    baking chocolate
1 tablespoon butter
1 (12-ounce) can evaporated milk

Mix the sugar, cornstarch and salt together. Combine the chocolate with the butter in a double boiler. Melt over simmering water, stirring to blend well. Whisk in the sugar mixture. Add the evaporated milk and cook until heated through and smooth, whisking constantly; the sauce will thicken as it cools.

Serves 8

FUDGE SYRUP

1 cup baking cocoa
1 cup sugar
1 cup skim milk
1 egg, lightly beaten
2 (1-tablespoon) pieces
    unsalted butter
1 teaspoon vanilla extract

Combine the baking cocoa and sugar in a large saucepan, mixing until no lumps remain. Add the milk and egg and mix well. Bring just to a boil over very low heat, stirring constantly. Let cool slightly. Stir in the butter until melted. Add the vanilla and let cool to room temperature. Store, covered, in the refrigerator for up to several weeks.

Serves 6

The twenty-five college graduates who were trained at the IBM Schoolhouse for three months as systems service women are shown here with three instructors at their 1935 graduation in Endicott, New York. The women were later assigned to IBM branch offices to assist salesmen in assessing customer requirements and to teach the customer's employees how to use their new IBM equipment.

brunch, snacks & beverages

Members of the IBM baseball team in 1938.

SPORTS LEAGUES

IBM sports leagues date back to the early 1900s. IBMers and their children are enthusiastic participants in different sports all over the world. Whether it is golf, baseball, basketball, bowling, soccer, or any other of the vast array of options, IBM teams fill the fields with IBM spectators cheering for them. The highlight of the year is the Watson Trophy dinner, where executives distribute awards and famous guest speakers join in the festivities. Sporting events continue to keep IBMers moving in their off-hours.

Chocolate French Toast 166

Chocolate Chip Waffles 166

Chocolate Banana Bread 167

Chocolate Banana Nut Bread 167

Double Chocolate Scones
with Cinnamon Butter 168

Mole Poblano 169

Chocolate-Drizzled Strawberries 170

Fruit Sticks with
Chocolate Sauce 170

Chocolate Popcorn Balls 171

White Chocolate-Covered
Popcorn 171

Chocolate-Dipped
Pretzel Snacks 172

White Chocolate Party Mix 174

Adults Only S'Mores 175

Fudgesicles 177

Chocolate Chip-Cream
Cheese Ball 177

Hot Coco-Choco 178

Mexican Hot Chocolate 179

Peanut Butter
Hot Chocolate 179

Toffee Hot Chocolate 180

New York Chocolate
Egg Cream 180

Budget Instant Cocoa Mix 182

Frozen Mudslide 182

Mexican Cocoa-Coffee 183

Chocolate Coconut
Martini 183

Chocolate Ice
Cream Martini 184

CHOCOLATE FRENCH TOAST

6 eggs
2 cups milk
1 tablespoon sugar
1 teaspoon vanilla extract
1/2 teaspoon salt
1/4 cup (1/2 stick) butter
8 diagonal slices French bread
4 milk chocolate candy bars
Strawberry sauce, raspberry sauce
   or chocolate syrup

Combine the eggs, milk, sugar, vanilla and salt in a bowl and beat until smooth. Melt half the butter in a nonstick skillet and heat over medium-high heat. Dip 4 slices of the bread in the egg mixture and place in the skillet. Cook for 5 minutes or until golden brown. Turn the bread over and place 1 chocolate bar on each slice of bread.

Dip the remaining 4 slices of bread in the egg mixture and place on the bread in the skillet; press firmly with a spatula. Cook for 5 minutes or until golden brown. Add the remaining butter to the skillet if needed and turn the toast over. Cook for 5 minutes or until golden brown. Remove to serving plates and drizzle with strawberry sauce, raspberry sauce or chocolate syrup.

Serves 4

CHOCOLATE CHIP WAFFLES

2 cups all-purpose flour
1/2 cup sugar
1 teaspoon baking soda
1/2 teaspoon salt
3 eggs
1 cup (2 sticks) butter, melted
   or softened
1 1/2 cups milk
1 teaspoon vanilla extract
1 cup (6 ounces) chocolate chips

Mix the flour, sugar, baking soda and salt in a bowl. Add the eggs, butter, milk and vanilla gradually, mixing until smooth. Stir in the chocolate chips.

Spoon the amount of batter recommended by the waffle iron directions onto a preheated waffle iron. Cook until golden brown. Repeat with the remaining batter.

Serves 4

CHOCOLATE BANANA BREAD

Mash the bananas in a large bowl. Add the flour, sugar, baking soda, salt and egg and mix well. Add the butter and mix just until moistened.

Spoon the batter into a greased loaf pan and sprinkle with the chocolate chips. Bake in a preheated 325-degree oven for 1 hour and 10 minutes or until a wooden pick inserted near the center comes out clean. Cool in the pan on a wire rack for 5 minutes and remove to the wire rack to cool completely.

Serves 8

3 overripe bananas
$1^1/2$ cups all-purpose flour
1 cup sugar
$1/2$ teaspoon baking soda
Pinch of salt
1 egg
$1/4$ cup ($1/2$ stick) butter or margarine, melted
$1/4$ cup ($1^1/2$ ounces) milk chocolate chips or "M & M's" Chocolate Candies

CHOCOLATE BANANA NUT BREAD

Cream the butter and sugar in a mixing bowl until light and fluffy, scraping the side of the bowl occasionally. Beat in the eggs, bananas, baking powder, baking soda and flour, scraping the side of the bowl frequently. Stir in the chocolate chips and nuts.

Spoon the batter into a 5×9-inch loaf pan sprayed with nonstick cooking spray. Bake in a preheated 350-degree oven for 60 to 70 minutes or until a wooden pick inserted near the center comes out clean. Cool in the pan on a wire rack for 15 minutes and remove to the wire rack to cool completely before slicing.

Serves 10

$1/2$ cup (1 stick) butter or margarine, softened
$1/2$ cup sugar
2 eggs
2 bananas, mashed
1 teaspoon baking powder
$3/4$ teaspoon baking soda
2 cups all-purpose flour
1 cup (6 ounces) chocolate chips
$1/2$ cup chopped nuts

DOUBLE CHOCOLATE SCONES WITH CINNAMON BUTTER

Scones

2 cups all-purpose flour

1/2 cup baking cocoa

1/3 cup packed light brown sugar

2 teaspoons baking powder

3/4 teaspoon baking soda

1/8 teaspoon salt

1/2 cup (1 stick) unsalted butter, chopped

1 cup (6 ounces) semisweet chocolate chips

1 egg

3/4 cup buttermilk

2 tablespoons granulated sugar

Cinnamon Butter

1/2 cup (1 stick) unsalted butter, softened

1/4 cup confectioners' sugar

1 teaspoon vanilla extract

1 teaspoon ground cinnamon

Scones

Combine the flour, baking cocoa, brown sugar, baking powder, baking soda and salt in a food processor. Add the butter and pulse to form coarse crumbs. Remove to a large bowl and stir in the chocolate chips.

Combine the egg and buttermilk in a small bowl and mix just until smooth. Add to the dry ingredients and mix just until the mixture comes together to form a dough. Divide the dough into two equal portions and place on a baking sheet lined with baking parchment. Press each portion into a flat round circle 6 inches in diameter. Cut each circle into six equal wedges, leaving the wedges in place and touching. Sprinkle with the granulated sugar.

Bake in a preheated 400-degree oven for 20 to 25 minutes or until the centers are firm to a light touch. Remove to a wire rack to cool slightly before separating the wedges.

Butter

Combine the butter, confectioners' sugar, vanilla and cinnamon in a small mixing bowl and beat until light and fluffy. Serve with the scone wedges.

Serves 12

MOLE POBLANO

Split the chiles and discard the seeds and veins; wash the hands after this step and take care not to touch the eyes. Melt half the lard in a large skillet and add the garlic, onions, plantain, anise, sesame seeds, raisins, cinnamon, cloves and pepper. Sauté over low heat until the garlic and onions are tender. Remove to a bowl with a slotted spoon. Add the chiles, tortillas, bread, peanuts and almonds to the drippings in the skillet and sauté lightly.

Place the chiles in a bowl with enough hot water to cover and let stand for 30 minutes; drain. Combine with the remaining sautéed ingredients in a food processor. Combine the chocolate with the hot turkey broth in a bowl and let stand until melted, stirring to blend well. Add enough of the broth mixture to the ingredients in the food processor to make a paste, processing until smooth.

Melt the remaining lard in a skillet. Add the puréed tomatoes and the paste. Cook over low to medium heat for 20 minutes, stirring constantly and adding sugar and salt to taste; the mixture should be thick.

Serve the mole over turkey or chicken, accompanied with white rice and beans, or over warm corn tortillas filled with cooked chicken and served with chopped onion, cheese and sour cream.

To prepare the broth, cook a turkey or 4 or 5 chickens in water with a large onion, half a garlic bulb and salt.

Serves 12

9 ounces (250 grams) pasilla chiles
9 ounces (250 grams) mulato chiles
14 ounces (400 grams) ancho chiles
10 1/2 ounces (300 grams) pork lard
5 garlic cloves, chopped
2 white onions, chopped
1 plantain, sliced
1 teaspoon liquid anise
5 ounces (150 grams) sesame seeds
5 ounces (150 grams) raisins
1/2 teaspoon ground cinnamon
4 cloves
1 teaspoon pepper
6 crisp corn tortillas, crushed
2 white deli rolls, crumbled
3 ounces (100 grams) peanuts
7 ounces (200 grams) skinless almonds
8 ounces chocolate (not sour)
2 cups turkey broth or chicken broth, heated
9 ounces (250 grams) tomatoes, braised, peeled and puréed
Sugar and salt to taste

CHOCOLATE-DRIZZLED STRAWBERRIES

1/2 cup (3 ounces) semisweet
    chocolate chips
2 teaspoons shortening
12 fresh strawberries

Combine the chocolate chips and shortening in a microwave-safe bowl. Microwave on High for 30 seconds and stir. Microwave in 15-second intervals until melted, stirring after each 15 seconds; watch carefully, as the chocolate will burn easily. Drizzle the mixture over the strawberries and let stand until the chocolate is set.

You can substitute dried apricots or strips of dried pineapple, mango or ginger for the fresh strawberries, dipping each halfway into the chocolate. You can also vary the recipe by using dark chocolate, milk chocolate, white chocolate or a combination. A 1-ounce square of melted chocolate will usually cover twelve pieces of dried fruit.

Makes 12

FRUIT STICKS WITH CHOCOLATE SAUCE

Strawberries, pineapple chunks,
    apple chunks, banana chunks,
    melon chunks, green grapes
    and/or marshmallows
1 cup whipping cream
8 ounces (1 1/3 cups) semisweet
    chocolate chips, or 6 ounces
    (1 cup) butterscotch chips and
    2 ounces (1/3 cup) semisweet
    chocolate chips

Thread the fruit onto eight skewers. Heat the cream in a saucepan over low heat. Add the chocolate chips and stir until the chocolate is melted and smooth.

Spoon the chocolate sauce into a fondue pot or a chocolate fountain. Dip the fruit skewers into the sauce.

Serves 8

CHOCOLATE POPCORN BALLS

Combine the chocolate chips, corn syrup and butter in a saucepan and bring to a boil. Pour over the popcorn and peanuts in a heatproof bowl and mix to coat evenly.

Let stand until cool enough to handle and shape into 3-inch balls. Store in an airtight container.

Serves 12

2 cups (12 ounces) semisweet
　　chocolate chips, dark chocolate
　　chips or milk chocolate chips
1 cup corn syrup
1/4 cup (1/2 stick) butter or
　　margarine
12 cups popped popcorn
1 (12-ounce) can peanuts, cashews
　　or macadamia nuts

WHITE CHOCOLATE-COVERED POPCORN

Pop the corn using the package directions; pour the popped corn from bowl to bowl to remove any uncooked kernels. Place the white chocolate chips in a microwave-safe bowl. Microwave on High for 2 minutes or until melted and smooth, stirring occasionally. Pour the chocolate over the popcorn in a heatproof bowl and mix well.

Spread the popcorn mixture in a single layer on a waxed paper-lined baking sheet. Let stand until cool; the mixture will have the consistency of brittle. Break into pieces to serve.

Serves 12

1 package natural popcorn
2 cups (12 ounces) white
　　chocolate chips

CHOCOLATE-DIPPED PRETZEL SNACKS

1 (10-ounce) package twist pretzels
5 cups granola cereal
5 cups crisp corn cereal
2 cups salted peanuts, walnuts or
    almonds, coarsely chopped
1 (16-ounce) package "M & M's"
    Chocolate Candies
3 tablespoons vegetable oil
4 cups (24 ounces) chocolate chips,
    white chocolate chips or
    butterscotch chips

Mix the pretzels, granola cereal, corn cereal, peanuts and "M & M's" in a heatproof bowl. Combine the oil and chocolate chips in a microwave-safe bowl. Microwave on Medium for 2 minutes, stirring after 1 minute. Microwave for 10 to 15 seconds longer or until smooth, stirring to blend well.

Pour the chocolate mixture over the cereal mixture and mix to coat evenly. Spread on three baking parchment-lined baking sheets and let stand until cool. Break into pieces and store in an airtight container.

Serves 5 to 6

Members of Berlin's IBM bowling team in 1957.

WHITE CHOCOLATE PARTY MIX

1 (10-ounce) package
    miniature pretzels
5 cups Cheerios
5 cups Corn Chex
2 cups roasted peanuts
1 (16-ounce) package plain
    "M & M's" Chocolate Candies
4 cups (24 ounces) white
    chocolate chips
3 tablespoons vegetable oil
1 teaspoon white vanilla extract

Combine the pretzels, Cheerios, Corn Chex, peanuts and "M & M's" in a large heatproof bowl. Combine the white chocolate chips with the oil in a microwave-safe bowl. Microwave on Medium for 2 minutes, stirring once. Add the vanilla and stir until smooth.

Pour the chocolate mixture over the cereal mixture and mix to coat well. Spread on waxed paper and let stand until cool. Break into pieces and store in an airtight container.

Serves 10 to 15

IBM France women's basketball team, circa 1950s.

ADULTS ONLY S'MORES

Place the graham crackers in a sealable plastic bag and break into 1-inch pieces. Combine the chocolate chips and peanut butter in a saucepan. Heat over low heat until the chocolate chips melt, stirring to blend well. Remove from the heat and stir to cool slightly. Add the marshmallows and graham cracker pieces, discarding the cracker crumbs; mix well.

Spread the mixture in a 10×18-inch pan sprayed with nonstick cooking spray; smooth the top with a spatula. Chill in the refrigerator for 1 hour or until firm. Cut into 48 bars. Store in an airtight container.

You can also add 1/2 cup toasted chopped pistachios or other nuts and/or 1/2 cup dried cranberries; for each add-in, increase the chocolate chips by 1 cup.

Makes 4 dozen

22 graham cracker squares
3 cups (18 ounces) dark
    chocolate chips
2 tablespoons peanut butter
3 cups miniature marshmallows

Mexico's IBM baseball team won its second consecutive championship in the Mexico City Insurance Company League, circa 1960s.

Mrs. Janusz Zaporski and the IBM volleyball team (back row) and opponents,
the Arpoador Praia Club (front row), Brazil, January 22, 1957.

FUDGESICLES

Combine the pudding mix, sugar, cream and milk in a bowl and mix using the pudding mix directions. Spoon into muffin cups or popsicle molds.

Freeze until partially firm. Insert a popsicle stick into each fudgesicle and freeze until firm.

Makes 6

1 (4-ounce) package chocolate
    instant pudding mix
1/2 cup sugar
1/2 cup cream
2 cups milk

CHOCOLATE CHIP-CREAM CHEESE BALL

Combine the cream cheese, confectioners' sugar, vanilla and cinnamon in a mixing bowl and beat until smooth. Stir in the chocolate chips.

Shape the cream cheese mixture into one large ball or two smaller balls and roll in the pecans, coating evenly. Chill for 30 minutes or longer. Serve with vanilla wafers, graham crackers, gingersnaps or miniature bagels.

Serves 15

24 ounces cream cheese, softened
1 cup confectioners' sugar
2 teaspoons vanilla extract
11/2 teaspoons ground cinnamon
2 cups (12 ounces) miniature
    chocolate chips
1 cup chopped pecans

HOT COCO-CHOCO

4 cups milk

1/2 cup heavy cream

6 tablespoons coconut cream

10 ounces bittersweet
  chocolate, chopped

1 teaspoon ground cinnamon

1 or 2 peppercorns (optional)

Whipped cream and dried coconut,
  for garnish

Combine the milk, heavy cream and coconut cream in a saucepan and heat just to the boiling point. Add the chocolate, cinnamon and peppercorns and reduce the heat.

Simmer for 8 to 10 minutes, stirring until the chocolate is melted and the mixture is smooth. Strain into mugs and garnish with whipped cream and dried coconut.

Serves 8 to 10

The IBM bowling team participating in the 1950 contest of the twilight bowling league in Buenos Aires, Argentina.

MEXICAN HOT CHOCOLATE

Melt the chocolate in a double boiler over simmering water. Combine the milk and cream in a saucepan and heat over medium heat; do not boil.

Pour a small amount of the hot milk mixture into the chocolate and stir to blend well. Stir in the remaining hot milk mixture. Add the sugar, cinnamon and vanilla and mix well. Heat over low heat for 3 minutes, beating at low speed or whisking constantly. Adjust the taste for cinnamon and vanilla. Serve in mugs.

Serves 4

2 ounces unsweetened
    baking chocolate
2 cups milk or reduced-fat milk
1 cup heavy cream or half-and-half
6 tablespoons sugar
1/2 to 1 teaspoon ground
    cinnamon, or 1 cinnamon stick
1 teaspoon vanilla extract, or
    1 vanilla bean

PEANUT BUTTER HOT CHOCOLATE

Place the milk in a small saucepan or microwave-safe bowl. Heat or microwave until heated through, skimming the surface if necessary. Add the chocolate syrup and peanut butter, stirring to blend well. Pour into a mug and garnish with whipped cream and chocolate sprinkles.

Serves 1

1 cup milk
2 to 4 teaspoons chocolate syrup
1 tablespoon peanut butter
Whipped cream and chocolate
    sprinkles, for garnish

TOFFEE HOT CHOCOLATE

4 cups milk
$1/2$ cup water
$1/2$ cup sugar
6 ounces bittersweet
    chocolate, chopped
$1/3$ cup (2 ounces)
    butterscotch chips
Whipped cream
1 toffee candy bar, crushed

Combine the milk, water and sugar in a saucepan and bring to a boil. Remove from the heat and add the chocolate and butterscotch chips; stir until the chocolate and butterscotch chips melt and the mixture is smooth. Pour into mugs and top with whipped cream and crushed candy.

Serves 4

NEW YORK CHOCOLATE EGG CREAM

1 cup milk
Sparkling seltzer water
3 tablespoons chocolate syrup

Pour the milk into a tall chilled glass and add sparkling water to fill. Stir in the chocolate syrup.

Serves 1

Sales and Administration Association soccer team, Buenos Aires, Argentina, 1941.

San Jose, California, IBMers enjoy a round of golf in the 1950s.

BUDGET INSTANT COCOA MIX

1 (16-ounce) package chocolate
   instant drink mix
1 (8-quart) package instant nonfat
   dry milk powder
1 (6-ounce) jar instant
   nondairy creamer
1 (1-pound) package confectioners'
   sugar, sifted

Combine the chocolate drink mix, nonfat dry milk, nondairy creamer
and confectioners' sugar in a bowl and whisk to mix well. Store in an
airtight container. Mix 1/3 cup of the mix with 3/4 cup hot water in a
mug for each serving, stirring to dissolve completely.

*For camping trips, measure 1-serving amounts into sealable plastic
bags labeled with the directions for making cocoa.*

Makes 48 cups

FROZEN MUDSLIDE

2 tablespoons vodka
2 tablespoons coffee liqueur
2 tablespoons Irish cream liqueur
2 to 3 scoops chocolate ice cream
   or vanilla ice cream

Combine the vodka, coffee liqueur, Irish cream liqueur and ice
cream in a blender. Blend at high speed until smooth. Pour into
a serving glass.

*You can increase the amounts, keeping the ratio of 1 part of
each liquid to 2 or 3 scoops of ice cream.*

Serves 1

MEXICAN COCOA-COFFEE

Combine the ground coffee, baking cocoa and cinnamon in the filter of a coffee maker. Add the water to the coffee maker and run through the brewing cycle. Pour 1 jigger of coffee liqueur into each of four mugs and fill the mugs with the brewed coffee. Garnish with whipped cream and cinnamon.

Serves 4

4 scoops (or more) ground
    coffee beans
1 tablespoon (heaping) baking cocoa
1/2 teaspoon ground cinnamon
4 cups water
4 (1-ounce) jiggers coffee liqueur
Whipped cream and ground
    cinnamon, for garnish

CHOCOLATE COCONUT MARTINI

Pour the vodka, chocolate liqueur, crème de cacao and Frangelico over ice in a cocktail shaker and shake to mix well. Strain into a chilled martini glass and top with flaked coconut.

Serves 1

1/4 cup vodka
2 tablespoons chocolate liqueur
1 splash of crème de cacao
1 splash of Frangelico
Flaked coconut

The IBM Club's soccer team in Germany, circa 1950s.

CHOCOLATE ICE CREAM MARTINI

1 large scoop chocolate ice cream
1 tablespoon Godiva white
    chocolate liqueur
Shaved dark chocolate, for garnish
1 small biscotto or chocolate
    mint cookie, for garnish

Place the ice cream in a martini glass and pour the liqueur over the ice cream. Garnish with shaved chocolate and a biscotto.

Serves 1

IBM Club bowling tournament, Manila, Philippines, May 1950.

ACKNOWLEDGMENTS

Kevin Sullivan
Director, IBM Workforce Relations

Sue Cutrone
Chairperson

RECIPE TEAM

Rayna Clifton
Chairperson

Mary Ann Hogan
Kathy Fusaro
Teri Wade

COMMUNICATIONS TEAM

Jaclyn Decicco
Chairperson

Randy Golden
Ellen Honeycutt
Bruce Moore
Jim Sinnochi
Jennifer Vickery

CORPORATE ARCHIVES

Stacy Fortner
Jennifer Halloran
Paul Lasewicz
Dawn Stanford

WINNER OF "COOKBOOK" TITLE CONTEST

Marcia Mealy

MARKETING AND DISTRIBUTION

Theresa Conway, *Co-Chairperson*
Valerie Cowing, *Co-Chairperson*
John Boden
Mark Couto
Sue McNamara
Mary-Ann O'Connor
Gisel Saia
Marilyn Spoon
Vinay K. Thazhatheveettil

CONTRIBUTORS

Annette Albro-Katz, Poughkeepsie, NY

Rose Adams, British Columbia, CA

Fatima Akhtar, Fairfax, GA

Geri Amaral, Jackson, GA

Maria Andrade, Cleveland, OH

Cynthia Anthofer, Denver, CO

Carol Arrigo, Armonk, NY

Susan Badar, Austin, TX

Megan Barry, Chicago, IL

Julie Baucom, Carpentersville, IL

Sandy Beall, Lansing, MI

Carla Bell, Creve Coeur, MO

Linda Biel, Somers, NY

Becky Birch, Seattle, WA

Diane Blakely, Hurley, NY

Robert Bolduc, Bethesda, MD

Debbie Branco, Westford, MA

Marc Brandfonbrener, Westford, MA

Desiree Briceno, Boca Raton, FL

Richard Calo, Armonk, NY

Ralph Calvano, Poughkeepsie, NY

Jo Cardone, Armonk, NY

Jodie Carson, Nashville, TN

Paula Cartelli, Boulder, CO

Donna Carter, Tulsa, OK

Angela Castleberry, Tulsa, OK

Diane Chalmers, Rochester, MN

Edith Chu, Cambridge, MA

Louise Clark, Tulsa, OK

Rayna Clifton, Poughkeepsie, NY

Janet Cohen, Milwaukee, WI

Debora Cole, Westford, MA

Jan Collins, Austin, TX

Alma Cui, Manila, Philippines

Sue Cutrone, Poughkeepsie, NY

Carol Cutts, Somers, NY

Cecilia D'Acunto, Buenos Aires, Argentina

Nicki Dankbar, Tulsa, OK

Cynthia Davis, Austin, TX

Pat Davis, Southfield, MI

Jaclyn Decicco, Somers, NY

Jeff Degler, Lexington, KY

Bernadette Del Bene, Armonk, NY

John Demarco, Fishkill, NY

Joseph Demarco, Fishkill, NY

Ronnie DiNucci, Armonk, NY

Christine Dodson, Lexington, KY

Pam Doepke, Minneapolis, MN

MaryKay Doheny, Bethesda, MD

Richard Dolezal, Atlanta, GA

MaryAnn Donovan, Rochester, MN

Kathy Eason, San Jose, CA

Stew Edelman, San Jose, CA

Debra Ellis, Watson, NY

Martha Ernst, Dayton, OH

Faith Erten, Izmir, Turkey

Marlys Fallen, Tulsa, OK

Mark Feblowitz, Cambridge, MA

David Felicione, Armonk, NY

Frank Fitzgerald, Poughkeepsie, NY

Sharon Fleisch, Atlanta, GA

Dee Fleming, Cambridge, MA

Sharon Forbes, Poughkeepsie, NY

Nancy Foxwell, Atlanta, GA

Brian Gegner, Des Moines, IA

Debbie Godwin, Austin, TX

Deborah Golestani, Poughkeepsie, NY

Sacha Goodson, Alpharetta, GA

Wendy Goshorn, Lexington, KY

Patricia Graves, Orlando, FL

Carolyn Green, Atlanta, GA

Andrew Leslie Griffiths, Burlington, VT

Kristine Guest, Atlanta, GA

Pawan Gupta, India

Patricia Gutierrez, Fairfax, VA

Kim Hansma, Lexington, KY

Sheree Harrell, Santa Rosa, CA

Diane Hartelius, Newark, NY

Lisa Hartung, Louisville, KY

Gillian Houghton, Winnipeg, CA

Sondra Iverson, Raleigh, NC

Janis Sewell Jackson, Menlo Park, CA

David Jewell, Lexington, KY

Luanne Jones, Houston, TX

J W Karol, Poughkeepsie, NY

Carla Kastelberg, Raleigh, NC

Sarah Katzenmaier, Lexington, KY
Heidi Kaufman, Somers, NY
Ross Ketterer, Lexington, KY
Bernard King-Smith, Poughkeepsie, NY
Karen Knight, Somers, NY
Mia Kovacs, Armonk, NY
Karthik Krishnaraj, Melbourne, Australia
Susan Lamberton, Poughkeepsie, NY
Jeff Laux, Boulder, CO
Steven Lebowitz, Bethesda, MD
Larry Leise, Raleigh, NC
Esther Linton, Raleigh, NC
Jodi MacCroy, Houston, TX
Heather Maki, Rochester, MN
Chuck & Renee Maniaci, Lansing, MI
Eileen Maroney, Charlotte, NY
Jamie Marshall, Tulsa, OK
Susan McKillip, Tulsa, OK
Dee Ann Millard, Minneapolis, MN
Laurie Miller, Boulder, CO
Teresa Morrow, Tulsa, OK
Stephanie Mounts, Olympia, WA
Brian Neugebauer, Poughkeepsie, NY
Teresa Ngo, San Jose, CA
Merideth Norris, Raleigh, NC
Glenda Nunn, Tulsa, OK
Lee O'Connor, Lansing, MN
Linda Odean, Rochester, MN
Donald Otis, Boulder, CO
Dawna O'Rourke, Atlanta, GA
Holly Pitt, Tulsa, OK
Val Pons, Kingston, NY
Sandhya Prabhakaran, Bangalore, India
Renee Di Prima Burns, Concord, MA
Brian Ragusa, Bedford, MA
Anna Mae Robbins, Poughkeepsie, NY
Paula Rogers, Tulsa, OK
F. Scott Romine, Dallas, TX
Jessica Rosman, Corol Gables, FL
Mary Jane Russell, Tulsa, OK
Linda Sander, Tulsa, OK
Mike Schmitt, Rochester, MN
Kim Shedlin, Armonk, NY

Pratibha Shetty, Bangalore, India
Nancy Shields, Cedar Park, TX
Robyn Howard Shriver, Highland Village, TX
Edward Simonds, Mechanicsburg, PA
Barbara Smallwood, Tulsa, OK
Kay Soltysiak, Cleveland, OH
Stuart Spillman, Tulsa, OK
Dale Stary, Poughkeepsie, NY
Diane Steelsmith, San Jose
Erma Stough, Essex Junction
Kevin Sullivan, Armonk, NY
Gabrijela Surkic, Austria
Shirley Swenson, Poughkeepsie, NY
Michele Szynal, Kingston, NY
Pam Tesch, Rochester, MN
Gayle Ternes, Tulsa, OK
Pam Tesch, Rochester, NY
Jill Thomson, Rochester, NY
Frances Timpanaro, Paramas, NJ
Kathy Trelatsky, Los Angeles, CA
Ed Trottier Essex, Junction, VT
Joanne Valente, Lexington, MA
Alda Valleri, Milano, Italy
Bonnie Van Volkinburg, Grand Rapids, MI
Joalva VandenBrink, Claremore, OK
Deborah Vannicola, Rome, Italy
Terri Wade, Akron, OH
Debbie Wastle, Victoria, BC, Canada
Patti Weigand, Mechanicsburg, PA
Donald Wells, Fishkill, NY
Linda West, Raleigh, NC
Lori Whisenhunt, Tulsa, OK
Jessica White, Atlanta, GA
Christine Winus, Yorktown, NY
Jackie Witkowski, Buffalo, NY
Jean Woitasek, Poughkeepsie, NY
Joanne Youlio, Poughkeepsie, NY
Karen Young, White Plains, NY
Ralph & Gloria Zimmerman, Hurley, NY
Beth Zonis, Waltham, MA
Roberto Zottar, Padova, Italy

INDEX

ACCOMPANIMENTS. *See also*
  Desserts, Sauces
  Cinnamon Butter, 168

ALMONDS
  Best-Ever English Toffee, 74
  Biscotti alla Pennacchi, 94
  Caprese, 17
  Chocolate Coconut Phyllo
    Triangles, 130
  Coconut Chocolate Almond
    Cheesecake, 138
  Cream Puff Dessert, 145
  Mole Poblano, 169

BANANA
  Chocolate Banana Bread, 167
  Chocolate Banana Nut Bread, 167
  Grandma's Icebox Dessert, 148

BEVERAGES
  Budget Instant Cocoa Mix, 182
  Hot Coco-Choco, 178
  Mexican Hot Chocolate, 179
  New York Chocolate
    Egg Cream, 180
  Peanut Butter Hot Chocolate, 179
  Toffee Hot Chocolate, 180

BEVERAGES, ALCOHOLIC
  Chocolate Coconut Martini, 183
  Chocolate Ice Cream
    Martini, 184
  Frozen Mudslide, 182
  Mexican Cocoa-Coffee, 183

BROWNIES
  Caramel Brownies, 86
  Chocolate Brownies, 86
  Chocolate Crunch Brownies, 87
  Kahlúa Fudge Brownies, 87
  Mom's 1950 Chocolate
    Brownies, 88
  White Chocolate Brownies, 88

BRUNCH
  Chocolate Banana Bread, 167
  Chocolate Banana Nut Bread, 167
  Chocolate Chip Waffles, 166
  Chocolate French Toast, 166
  Double Chocolate Scones with
    Cinnamon Butter, 168
  Hazelnut Biscotti, 94
  Mole Poblano, 169

BUTTERSCOTCH CHIPS
  Rocky Road Fudge, 66
  Snickers Fudge, 67
  Toffee Hot Chocolate, 180

CAKES, 1-LAYER
  Caprese, 17
  Chocolate Cake, 19
  Chocolate Crazy Cake, 20
  Cupavci, 20
  Devil's Black Cake, 21
  Flourless Chocolate Cake, 23
  Frozen Chocolate Cake, 23
  Indian Chocolate Cake, 26
  Rich Chocolate Cake, 25
  Sour Cream Chocolate
    Chip Cake, 19
  Sugar-Free Chocolate Cake, 27

CAKES, 2-LAYER
  Fudgy Chocolate Layer Cake, 14
  Mocha Layer Cake, 15

CAKES, 3-LAYER
  Swiss Chocolate Torte, 16

CAKES, 9×13
  Black Forest Cake, 33
  Chocolate Cherry Cake, 34
  Chocolate Chip Cake, 35
  Chocolate Chip Zucchini Cake, 36
  Chocolate Cinnamon
    Snacking Cake, 38
  Chocolate Mocha Cake, 35
  Chocolate Syrup Cake, 46
  Earthquake Cake, 38
  Frosted Chocolate Cake, 37
  Heavenly Cake, 41
  Hot Fudge Chocolate Cake, 40
  Mississippi Mud Cake, 42
  Navy Cake, 46
  Oatmeal Chocolate Chip Cake, 36
  One-Pan Peanut Butter
    Chocolate Cake, 43
  Screwball Dark Chocolate Cake, 43
  Triple Chocolate Cake, 47
  Wacky Cake, 44

CAKES, BUNDT
  Black Russian Cake, 29
  Chocolate Bundt Cake, 31
  Chocolate Coconut Fudge Ring
    Bundt Cake, 30
  Fabulous Chocolate-Chocolate
    Chip Cake, 29
  Mocha Bundt Cake, 32
  Prestigio Cake, 32
  Vanilla Wafer Cake, 30
  Vodka Cake, 33

CAKES, CAKE MIXES
  Black Russian Cake, 29
  Chocolate Bundt Cake, 31
  Chocolate Cherry Cake, 34

Chocolate Cherry Cupcakes, 51
Chocolate Chip Cake, 35
Earthquake Cake, 38
Fabulous Chocolate-Chocolate
  Chip Cake, 29
Heavenly Cake, 41
Hot Fudge Chocolate Cake, 40
Mocha Bundt Cake, 32
Surprise Cupcakes, 54
Swiss Chocolate Torte, 16
Triple Chocolate Cake, 47
Vodka Cake, 33

CAKES, CUPCAKES
  Chocolate Cherry Cupcakes, 51
  Macaroon-Filled Chocolate
    Cupcakes, 52
  Surprise Cupcakes, 54

CAKES, RAMEKINS
  Amazingly Rich Individual
    Chocolate Pudding Cakes, 50
  Chocolate Lava Cakes, 51

CAKES, SHEET
  Chocolate Sheet Cake, 47
  Texas Sheet Cake, 49

CAKES, SPRINGFORM
  Chocolate Mousse Cake, 24
  Chocolate Torte, 28
  Creole Chocolate Cake, 18
  Intensely Rich Chocolate
    Cake, 22
  Torta al Cioccolato, 17

CANDY
  Best-Ever English Toffee, 74
  Brigadeiro, 60
  Chocolate Clusters, 60
  Chocolate Flick, 61
  Chocolate Pizza, 73
  Cordial Cherries, 61
  German Chocolate Rum
    Clusters, 74
  Millionaire Candy, 69
  Peanut Butter Bonbons, 72
  Peanut Butter Chews, 71
  Texas Millionaires, 70

CANDY, FUDGE
  Chocolate Cheese
    Fudge, 62
  Chocolate Fudge, 62
  Fantasy Fudge, 64
  Foolproof Fudge, 64
  Layered Mint Fudge, 66
  Rocky Road Fudge, 66
  Snickers Fudge, 67

CANDY, TRUFFLES
Chocolate Peanut Butter Truffles, 80
Chocolate Raspberry Truffles, 76
Chocolate Truffles, 77
Oreo Truffles, 77
Truffles with a Twist, 79
White Chocolate Avocado Truffles, 80

CHEESECAKES
Chocolate Mint Swirl Cheesecake
 with Chocolate Nut Crust, 141
Chocolate Peppermint
 Cheesecake, 142
Chocolate Zebra Cheesecake, 144
Coconut Chocolate Almond
 Cheesecake, 138
Fudge Truffle Cheesecake, 139
Killer Chocolate Cheesecake, 140
Triple Chocolate Cheesecake, 143

CHERRY
Black Forest Cake, 33
Black Forest Cookies, 95
Chocolate Cherry Cake, 34
Chocolate Cherry Cupcakes, 51
Chocolate Pizza, 73
Cordial Cherries, 61

CHOCOLATE CHIPS, BRUNCH
Chocolate Banana Bread, 167
Chocolate Banana Nut Bread, 167
Chocolate Chip Waffles, 166
Double Chocolate Scones with
 Cinnamon Butter, 168

CHOCOLATE CHIPS, CAKES
Black Forest Cake, 33
Chocolate Bundt Cake, 31
Chocolate Chip Cake, 35
Chocolate Chip Zucchini Cake, 36
Chocolate Cinnamon
 Snacking Cake, 38
Fabulous Chocolate-Chocolate
 Chip Cake, 29
Mocha Bundt Cake, 32
Oatmeal Chocolate Chip Cake, 36
Sour Cream Chocolate
 Chip Cake, 19
Surprise Cupcakes, 54
Triple Chocolate Cake, 47
Vanilla Wafer Cake, 30

CHOCOLATE CHIPS, CANDY
Chocolate Clusters, 60
Chocolate Flick, 61
Chocolate Fudge, 62
Chocolate Pizza, 73
Fantasy Fudge, 64
Foolproof Fudge, 64

Layered Mint Fudge, 66
Millionaire Candy, 69
Peanut Butter Bonbons, 72
Rocky Road Fudge, 66
Snickers Fudge, 67
Texas Millionaires, 70

CHOCOLATE CHIPS, COOKIES
Biscotti alla Pennacchi, 94
Black Forest Cookies, 95
Buckaroons, 96
Caramel Brownies, 86
Chocolate Brownie Cookies, 96
Chocolate Brownies, 86
Chocolate Chip Cookies, 97
Chocolate Chip Shortbread, 91
Chocolate Crunch Brownies, 87
Chocolate Macaroon Squares, 93
Chocolate Mint Sugar Cookies, 104
Cracker Brittle, 101
First-Prize Chocolate Mint
 Cookies, 103
Hazelnut Biscotti, 94
Magic Bars, 93
Peanut Butter Squares, 91
Pizzelle, 109

CHOCOLATE CHIPS, CRUSTS
Chocolate Chip Crust, 144
Chocolate Nut Crust, 141

CHOCOLATE CHIPS, DESSERTS
Chocolate-Drizzled Strawberries, 170
Chocolate Meltdown, 158
Chocolate Mess, 148
Coconut Chocolate Almond
 Cheesecake, 138
Fruit Sticks with
 Chocolate Sauce, 170
Fudge Truffle Cheesecake, 139
Healthy Chocolate Mousse, 153
Manitoba "Moose" Chocolate
 Pudding, 153

CHOCOLATE CHIPS, FILLINGS
Coconut Chocolate Chip Filling, 30

**CHOCOLATE CHIPS, FROSTINGS/GLAZES/
 TOPPINGS**
Creamy Frosting, 14
Fudgy Frosting, 34

CHOCOLATE CHIPS, PASTRIES
Choco-Baklava, 129

CHOCOLATE CHIPS, PIES
Chocolate Marvel Pie, 121
Chocolate Peanut Butter
 Cookie Pie, 127

Chocolate Peanut Butter Pie, 124
Chocolate Pecan Pie, 127
Chocolate Pie, 114
Chocolate Silk Pie, 128
Fudge Walnut Brownie Pie, 120

CHOCOLATE CHIPS, SNACKS
Adults Only S'Mores, 175
Chocolate Chip-Cream
 Cheese Ball, 177
Chocolate-Dipped
 Pretzel Snacks, 172
Chocolate-Drizzled
 Strawberries, 170
Chocolate Popcorn Balls, 171
Fruit Sticks with Chocolate
 Sauce, 170

COCONUT
Chocolate Chunk Macadamia
 Cookies, 103
Chocolate Clusters, 60
Chocolate Coconut Coating, 20
Chocolate Coconut Martini, 183
Chocolate Coconut Phyllo
 Triangles, 130
Chocolate-Dipped Coconut
 Macaroons, 98
Chocolate Macaroon
 Squares, 93
Chocolate Pizza, 73
Chocolate Walnut
 Squares, 92
Coconut Chocolate Almond
 Cheesecake, 138
Coconut Chocolate Chip
 Filling, 30
Coconut Filling, 32, 52
Cream Puff Dessert, 145
Earthquake Cake, 38
Macaroon-Filled Chocolate
 Cupcakes, 52
Magic Bars, 93
Mississippi Mud Cake, 42
One-Minute Cookies, 105
Vanilla Wafer Cake, 30

COFFEE
Chocolate Cinnamon
 Snacking Cake, 38
Chocolate Mocha Cake, 35
Chocolate Sauce, 160
Chocolate Silk Pie, 128
Chocolate Torte, 28
Mexican Cocoa-Coffee, 183
Mocha Frosting, 15
Mocha Layer Cake, 15
Mocha Slice Cookies, 105
Truffles with a Twist, 79

COOKIES. *See also* Brownies;
   Frostings/Glazes/Toppings
Biscotti alla Pennacchi, 94
Chocolate Krispies, 98
Cracker Brittle, 101
Hazelnut Biscotti, 94
Mocha Slice Cookies, 105
Pizzelle, 109

COOKIES, BARS
Chocolate Chip Shortbread, 91
Chocolate Macaroon Squares, 93
Chocolate Walnut Squares, 92
Crème de Menthe Squares, 89
Fudge Bars, 90
Ghirardelli Classic White Chip
   Macadamia Bars, 92
Magic Bars, 93
Peanut Butter Squares, 91

COOKIES, CAKE MIXES
Caramel Brownies, 86
Easy Chocolate Butter Cookies, 97

COOKIES, DROP
Black Forest Cookies, 95
Buckaroons, 96
Chewy Milk Chocolate
   Oatmeal Cookies, 107
Chocolate and Oatmeal
   Peanut Butter Cookies, 107
Chocolate Brownie Cookies, 96
Chocolate Chip Cookies, 97
Chocolate Chunk Macadamia
   Cookies, 103
Chocolate-Dipped Coconut
   Macaroons, 98
Easy Chocolate Nut Drops with
   Creamy Fudge Frosting, 106
One-Minute Cookies, 105

COOKIES, SHAPED
Brownie Balls, 101
Chocolate Krinkles, 102
Chocolate Mint Sugar Cookies, 104
Easy Chocolate Butter Cookies, 97
First-Prize Chocolate Mint
   Cookies, 103
Kiss Cookies, 100
Old-Fashioned Chocolate
   Cookie Snaps, 109

CRUSTS
Chocolate Butter Crust, 143
Chocolate Chip Crust, 144
Chocolate Cookie Crust, 138
Chocolate Crumb Crust, 140
Chocolate Graham Cracker
   Crust, 89

Chocolate Nut Crust, 141
Chocolate Wafer Crust, 22, 142
Vanilla Wafer Crust, 139

DESSERT PASTRIES
Choco-Baklava, 129
Chocolate Coconut Phyllo
   Triangles, 130
Fondant Pastry, 131
Fudge Brownie Cups, 132
White Chocolate Mousse
   Pastries, 133

DESSERTS. *See also* Cakes; Candy;
   Cheesecakes; Cookies; Pies
Adults Only S'Mores, 175
Butterfinger Dessert, 145
Chocolate-Drizzled Strawberries, 170
Chocolate Gravy, 159
Chocolate Meltdown, 158
Chocolate Mess, 148
Cream Puff Dessert, 145
Creepy Mud Dessert, 159
Devil's Float, 146
Fruit Sticks with
   Chocolate Sauce, 170
Girdle Buster, 146
Grandma's Icebox Dessert, 148
Meringue Filled with
   Chocolate and Nuts, 149
Mexican Chocolate Icebox
   Dessert, 147

DESSERTS, CAKE MIXES
Chocolate Kahlúa Trifle, 156
Chocolate Mess, 148
Chocolate Pudding Trifle, 155
Chocolate Trifle, 156

DESSERTS, MOUSSE
Chocolate Mousse with
   Frangelico, 150
Dark and White Chocolate
   Mousse, 150
Healthy Chocolate Mousse, 153
Three-Chocolate Ice Cream
   Mousse, 152

DESSERTS, PUDDINGS
Four-Three-Two-One
   Chocolate Pudding, 155
Manitoba "Moose"
   Chocolate Pudding, 153

DESSERTS, SAUCES
Chocolate Sauce, 160
Fudge Syrup, 160
Hot Fudge Sauce, 160
Strawberry Sauce, 152

DESSERTS, TRIFLES
Brownie Trifle, 158
Chocolate Kahlúa Trifle, 156
Chocolate Pudding Trifle, 155
Chocolate Trifle, 156

FILLINGS
Chocolate Filling, 149
Coconut Chocolate Chip
   Filling, 30
Coconut Filling, 32, 52
Crème de Menthe Filling, 89

FROSTINGS/GLAZES/TOPPINGS
Almond Crunch Frosting, 16
Chocolate Coconut Coating, 20
Chocolate Cream Frosting, 25
Chocolate Frosting Sauce, 32
Chocolate Glaze, 22, 27
Chocolate Peanut Butter
   Frosting, 55
Chocolate Sheet Cake, 47
Chocolate Whipped Cream, 24
Confectioners' Sugar
   Frosting, 37
Cooked Fudge Frosting, 88
Creamy Frosting, 14
Creamy Fudge Frosting, 106
Fudge Frosting, 54
Fudgy Frosting, 34
Fudgy Topping, 40
Kahlúa Glaze, 29
Mississippi Mud Frosting, 42
Mocha Frosting, 15
Orange Topping, 31
Rich Topping, 50
Sheet Cake Frosting, 47
Texas Sheet Cake Frosting, 49
Wacky Frosting, 44

FRUIT. *See also* Banana; Cherry;
   Coconut; Raspberry; Strawberry
Fruit Sticks with Chocolate
   Sauce, 170

HAZELNUTS
Chocolate Mousse Cake, 24
Hazelnut Biscotti, 94

MACADAMIA NUTS
Chocolate Chunk Macadamia
   Cookies, 103
Ghirardelli Classic White Chip
   Macadamia Bars, 92

NUTS. *See also* Almonds; Hazelnuts;
   Macadamia Nuts; Peanuts;
   Pecans; Walnuts
Indian Chocolate Cake, 26

PASTRIES
  Pastry, 131
  Phyllo, 129

PEANUT BUTTER. *See also* Pies,
    Peanut Butter
  Adults Only S'Mores, 175
  Chocolate and Oatmeal
    Peanut Butter Cookies, 107
  Chocolate Crunch Brownies, 87
  Chocolate Flick, 61
  Chocolate Peanut Butter Frosting, 55
  Chocolate Peanut Butter Truffles, 80
  Kiss Cookies, 100
  One-Minute Cookies, 105
  One-Pan Peanut Butter
    Chocolate Cake, 43
  Peanut Butter Bonbons, 72
  Peanut Butter Chews, 71
  Peanut Butter Hot Chocolate, 179
  Peanut Butter Squares, 91
  Rocky Road Fudge, 66
  Snickers Fudge, 67

PEANUTS
  Chocolate-Dipped
    Pretzel Snacks, 172
  Chocolate Pizza, 73
  Chocolate Popcorn Balls, 171
  Mole Poblano, 169
  Peanut Butter Chews, 71
  Snickers Fudge, 67
  White Chocolate Party Mix, 174

PECANS
  Chocolate Chip-Cream
    Cheese Ball, 177
  Chocolate Krinkles, 102
  Chocolate Macaroon
    Squares, 93
  Chocolate Pecan Pie, 127

  Girdle Buster, 146
  Kahlúa Fudge Brownies, 87
  Millionaire Candy, 69
  Texas Millionaires, 70

PIES. *See also* Crusts; Pastries
  Chocolate Almond Pie, 114
  Chocolate Marvel Pie, 121
  Chocolate Mousse Pie, 122
  Chocolate Pecan Pie, 127
  Chocolate Pie, 114
  Chocolate Silk Pie, 128
  Creamy Chocolate Mousse Pie, 125
  Fudge Walnut Brownie Pie, 120
  Grandmother's Chocolate Pie, 118
  Hot Fudge Pie, 118
  Triple-Layer Mud Pie, 125

PIES, CHESS
  Chocolate Chess Pie, 116
  Southern Chocolate Chess Pie, 117

PIES, PEANUT BUTTER
  Chocolate Peanut Butter
    Cookie Pie, 127
  Chocolate Peanut Butter Pie, 124

RASPBERRY
  Chocolate Raspberry Truffles, 76
  Sugar-Free Chocolate Cake, 27

SNACKS
  Adults Only S'Mores, 175
  Chocolate Chip-Cream
    Cheese Ball, 177
  Chocolate-Dipped
    Pretzel Snacks, 172
  Chocolate-Drizzled Strawberries, 170
  Chocolate Popcorn Balls, 171
  Fruit Sticks with
    Chocolate Sauce, 170

  Fudgesicles, 177
  White Chocolate-Covered
    Popcorn, 171
  White Chocolate Party Mix, 174

STRAWBERRY
  Chocolate-Drizzled Strawberries, 170
  Creole Chocolate Cake, 18
  Strawberry Sauce, 152

WALNUTS
  Best-Ever English Toffee, 74
  Choco-Baklava, 129
  Chocolate Brownies, 86
  Chocolate Nut Crust, 141
  Chocolate Sheet Cake Frosting, 47
  Chocolate Walnut Squares, 92
  Foolproof Fudge, 64
  Fudge Walnut Brownie Pie, 120
  Magic Bars, 93
  Oatmeal Chocolate Chip Cake, 36

WHITE CHOCOLATE
  Chocolate Meltdown, 158
  Chocolate Zebra Cheesecake, 144
  Dark and White Chocolate
    Mousse, 150
  Ghirardelli Classic White Chip
    Macadamia Bars, 92
  Layered Mint Fudge, 66
  Peanut Butter Chews, 71
  Three-Chocolate Ice Cream
    Mousse, 152
  White Chocolate Avocado Truffles, 80
  White Chocolate Brownies, 88
  White Chocolate-Covered
    Popcorn, 171
  White Chocolate Mousse
    Pastries, 133
  White Chocolate Party Mix, 174

Image Copyrights

For additional copies of

BEYOND *chips*

Internal: w3.ibm.com/ibmclub/ibmclub.nsf
Lotus ID: ibmclub/armonk/ibm

Retirees: www.ibm.com/ibm/ibmclub

IBM club

Great people. Great company.

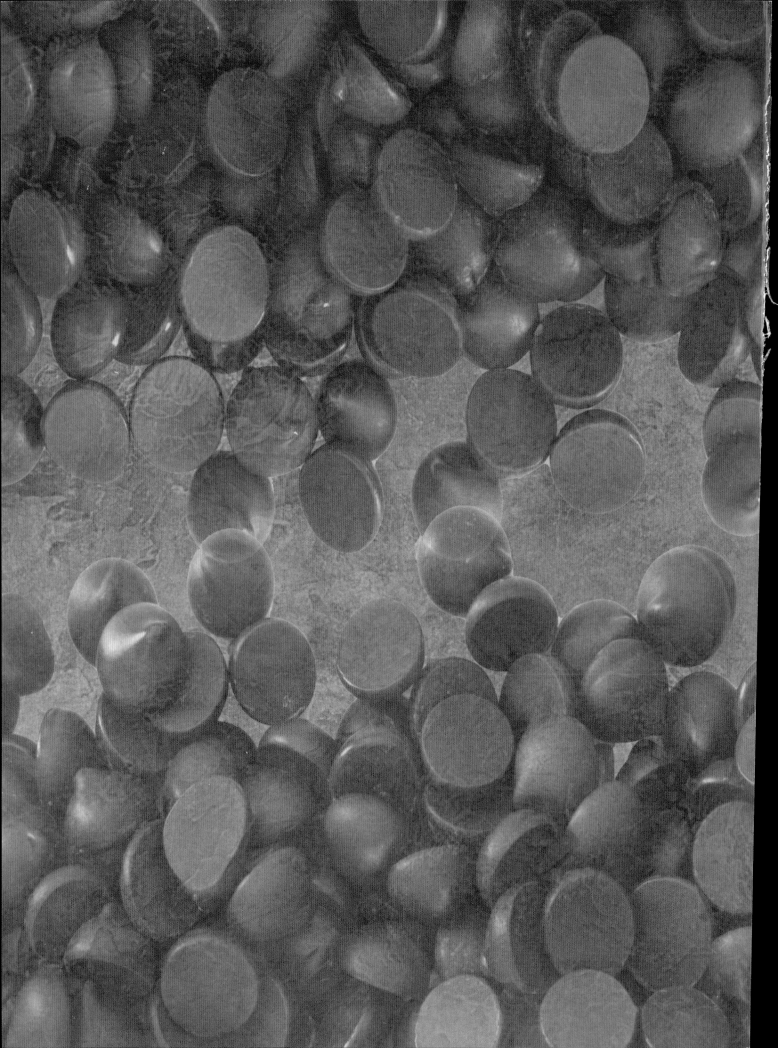